Making It in Management

Making It in Management

Developing the Thinking You Need to Move Up the Organization Ladder … and Stay There

LAWRENCE ANDERSON, PhD

iUniverse, Inc.
Bloomington

Making It in Management
Developing the Thinking You Need to Move Up the Organization Ladder ... and
Stay There

iUniverse books may be ordered through booksellers or by contacting:

iUniverse
1663 Liberty Drive
Bloomington, IN 47403
www.iuniverse.com
1-800-Authors (1-800-288-4677)

ISBN: 978-1-4620-3520-5 (sc)
ISBN: 978-1-4620-3521-2 (ebk)

Printed in the United States of America

iUniverse rev. date: 08/03/2011

Praise for Making It in Management

Making It in MANAGEMENT is a bonus for managers and leaders who desire upward mobility. It will give them a tremendous body of knowledge to help them prepare for the future. And while the book contains value for the target group – those who aren't at the top yet – it also offers existing leaders an opportunity to gauge their current practices against Dr. Anderson's well-documented and practical concepts. The personal exercises at the end of each chapter add considerable value to the 'staying power' of the book. These will enable managers to take-away the essential know-how that will help get the recognition they need to move up the corporate ladder.

Daniel Stamp, Chairman, Priority Management Systems International, Vancouver, Canada

"Our corporate relationship with Larry Anderson over many years has imparted a wealth of managerial knowledge to our employees. His book *Making It in MANAGEMENT* embodies invaluable knowledge for all."

Jim Dadd, Manager Corporate Development A.R. Thomson Group, BC

"Larry Anderson has been my organization development consultant-of-choice for many years. The topics in his new book *Making It in MANAGEMENT* are ideal for both aspiring managers and existing senior managers; both will benefit from his practical experiences."

Linda Shales, Consultant (and former VP Human Resources)

To Carol
. . . for everything and more

Foreword

At last count, after a career of thirty-five years (and counting), I've been privileged to conduct over one hundred and fifty client assignments for diverse organizations worldwide. They were large and small, private and public and all involved *organization change.* Several common themes were evident in most of these organizations: they had goals to achieve and most often the resources to get them there. But there were usually organizational "issues" that hampered the attainment of these ultimate goals, most of which were rationalized as typical of large organizations. As long as there was enough profit being realized, these "issues" were tolerated; but when business was down and margins were lean and the mention of survival troublesome, actions were finally taken to mitigate potential damage. Some of the actions worked; some didn't. People looked to management for the answers and these answers were not always forthcoming because the predominant focus and expertise of management was on the marketplace and the products or services and not enough on the organization itself, i.e. the *organization's effectiveness, or "health."*

My introduction to management consulting was accidental. I was headhunted by one of the "Big-Eight" firms (at that time) on behalf of one of their clients who needed a senior HR leader. Up to that point, I had gained solid experience working for major organizations including Westinghouse, Ford Motor Company and the Government of Ontario. My experience covered the waterfront of HR: Recruiting, Compensation, Labor Relations, Training and whatever else came along within those unionized organizations, not excluding dealing with conflict. Before discovering my passion for organization change consulting, I used to wonder why my own organizations went through cycles of expansion and retrenchment. It seemed odd to me that individual functions could be performing well yet, overall, the organization's leaders were dissatisfied with corporate results. As an HR person at the time, I viewed success through my biased HR prism. If human performance was okay (I thought) what else was causing lack-luster performance? Was there something unclear about our strategy? Did the company leaders misread the market and the competition? Were our products and services still in demand? Did our bosses know where the new growth areas would be? Did our overall structure facilitate decision-making and provide for accountability? Were we using up-to-date processes to optimize efficiency? Were our people productive and satisfied, or could they or should they be doing more? Were there things about our workplace conditions that were limiting optimal results? I had read about *organization culture* at university but it seemed too abstract a concept then to appreciate its overall significance in determining organization effectiveness.

To my surprise (and everlasting pleasure), my new "Big Eight" partner challenged me to exchange my HR-biased view of each client organization and broaden it to be able to examine the overall fit between the interdependent variables of strategy, structure, processes, people, climate and culture. Thus began my avid interest in a fundamental question: *What makes an organization work?* And my partner was right: almost every client of ours was a member of senior management, if not the CEO, and each would seek our opinion on the causes of current *organization* performance. That cured me of one-dimensional viewing. It wasn't just a marketing problem or a leadership issue or a morale problem or a product or service issue. Neither was it just the new IT system that was installed nor the aged equipment that people were forced to use. It was more than that. It was an *organization problem* in the fullest sense of the term.

The consulting profession hastened my enthusiasm for a more *holistic* sense of organizational behavior. I began teaching at my local college, focusing on Organizational Behavior as my specialty. I became an adjunct professor at two universities and continued to teach over the next thirty years in parallel with my consulting business. After a fulfilling experience as a manager in my premier management consulting firms, I formed my own firm in Toronto, Canada, and spent the next twenty-five years dealing with organization change across Canada, in the USA and overseas in Ghana, United Arab Emirates, Indonesia, Zimbabwe and Zaire. These clients had a common desire for survival and growth. They also had common obstacles, chief of which were *internal* by nature, yet curable with insight.

- Senior management in one organization sought my input on their declining organization performance. They were losing market share and profit margins were dropping. Reacting to stop further damage, they threw overtime at their production capacity while arbitrarily increasing quotas. They made no changes to the existing organization structure. Things got worse; employees reacted with feigned effort, a few vulnerable managers were dismissed and draconian cost controls were imposed with little effect. There was the familiar blame game within management where no one accepted responsibility for failing performance. I was hired to perform an organizational audit involving private interviews and anonymous surveys with a cross-section of employees from all levels. The results were not confidential but the anonymity of the interviewees was (a sacred rule for an external consultant). The results made the situation clear in terms of causes-and-effects: strategically, the market had changed and current products were not in the same demand as in past years. New markets and/or new products and services had to be created. There were countless weaknesses in the design of the organization and the pinpointing of accountability. The review produced half a dozen priorities for improved efficiency and a current list of legitimate employee concerns. Before our strategic planning exercises, top management had overlooked the strategy of growing market share by buying-out competitors and/or adding new products and services. This new strategy was the beginning of organizational change. Management now turned their attention to the essential organization changes that were needed to implement the new strategy and enable the company to survive the transition period. Sharing the new direction, employees were engaged in sessions on how to implement the new strategy, especially ways and means of doing it efficiently while making the work climate more productive and satisfying. In this case, the organization as-a-whole was considered part of the change.

- As a former training manager at Ford Motor Company, I had developed a series of practical workshops aimed at increasing the conceptual knowledge of our supervisors and managers on how organizations work! In too many client organizations a large percentage of managers remain focused on their immediate functional goals (effects) without considering too deeply the factors that were contingent on their success (causes). To no one's surprise, many of these causes were organizational in nature. When I became an adjunct professor, I was asked to teach Organization Behavior. That was an eye-opener for me and became the core emphasis of my professional practice which included workshops for client managers to emphasize the importance of organization effectiveness. Here are a few of the more impactful topics:

- Creating your unit's business *strategy* and keeping it on track.
- Providing *structure* to achieve both effectiveness and efficiency.
- Finding ways to increase efficiency through improved *systems and processes.*
- Creating the conditions for *human resource* productivity and satisfaction
- Creating a work *climate* where people want to their best and stay.
- Choosing and safe-guarding *cultural values* that guide ethical conduct.

More often than I expected, clients attending my leadership/ management workshops would approach me and say something like this: "Why don't you write a book about the topics we covered . . . one that makes it easy to understand . . . like in this workshop?" These reminders have led me to the conclusion that while technical/

functional learning abounds in organizations, there is a need for more learning around how the *organization itself* works. I've always been flattered by participant suggestions to write such a book but too preoccupied to act. Finally, suggestion and opportunity meet.

I decided to focus on managers who aren't at the top of the management structure yet because, as a middle-manager in my pre-consulting roles in manufacturing and government, I found the role fuzzy. I remember my first promotion above the supervisory level. When I asked my boss for an outline of my responsibilities, his reply was surprising: "Why don't we wait six months to a year and see how the job develops!" So, for quite some time, my job seemed dictated by what came up from below or what came down from above. Even more confusing were surprise demands made on my group by lateral departments because of the horizontal handoffs forced by the functional silo structures. I described my job as a default manager.

For a year, my job consisted of spending too much time doing what I had done at the previous level, no doubt duplicating the work of my direct reports. But that was what I knew I knew. As for my new job, I didn't know what I didn't know. I wondered about my supposed added-value role. So did my direct reports. They tested me by delegating work up . . . especially the unpleasant tasks, and I, not knowing any better and wishing to help them, obliged. I had created my own monster. To complicate matters further, my VP and his cohorts reminded me that I was an operations guy and that the heady stuff, the strategic direction of the organization as well as business and culture development, was theirs.

The senior managers seemed to operate on the notion that withheld information is power, something that only they could possess or be trusted to hold. I spent more and more time doing my old job and less and less time looking at what my bosses were doing above me. It all seemed hush-hush. I heard the word 'strategic' used so often that I never acquired a proper understanding of its meaning until I became a management consultant and started working the concept, seriously. As I look back, the word "strategic" was jargon; used too often yet meaning little. I thought the roles at the executive level were kept deliberately mysterious; thus, middle managers preparing to move upward had very little to go on as far as career preparation was concerned. Doing a good job and waiting (and hoping) seemed to be the primary modes of preparing to move up.

As the title of my book *Making It in Management* suggests, I want to include the topics that I have found will help prepare managers to either go *up* in their current organizations, or *out and up* in someone else's. Before choosing the chapter topics I kept coming back to three central questions that were posed to me and once answered, made a huge difference in my appreciation of management's role in creating an organization's strategy. I still meet middle managers to whom the following questions have not been put (to their detriment). Answering them is important groundwork for preparing for their next career moves in management. Obviously there are other important questions related to moving upward, but until I struggled with these broader ones, I didn't 'see' the actions I needed to take to progress. Here are my favorite questions middle managers should consider:

1. If my direct reports, especially my supervisors and team leaders, are all doing their jobs satisfactorily, what is my unique added-value role to support them?
2. If I can answer Question 1 correctly, then what additional knowledge and skills must I develop personally in order to become a high-potential candidate for management positions above me?
3. After I've figured out the improvements I need to make in my technical, human-relations and management conceptual-skills repertoire, how do I feel about myself? Do I possess high self-esteem? Do I have confidence and a well-defined purpose; feel a strong sense of responsibility; am I assertive? Do I possess personal integrity? Am I worthy of higher responsibility?

In the following chapters each of these critical questions is addressed, partly with my opinions, partly from other subject experts and partly through self-mentoring exercises found at the end of each chapter. Questions 1 and 2 will help you understand your current position and what you'll need to do, professionally, to advance. The subject of Question 3, *you* as a person, is personal and remains the tie-breaker. As you finish each chapter, I urge you to complete the suggested exercises before moving to the next topic. If you do, you will see the context for actions that are required for your career advancement.

After facilitating several hundred well-received management/ leadership workshops and seminars over the years, plus a lot of on-site consulting assignments, I realized that much of management development is *self-development* accomplished with limited formal organizational help. That is why I encourage you to concentrate on the recommended exercises at the end of each chapter; completing them will help you begin your preparations for your next move while solidifying your reputation at the level you are now.

The topics I have chosen in the following chapters are my recommended 1, 2, 3's for middle managers, although most of these concepts and tips do apply at all levels. The difference is degree. But middle managers have one leg in the senior management door and the other at the supervisory door . . . . a part of neither, yet they are expected to be advocates for both. At the same time, middle managers are hoping for upward mobility. The three main themes I've chosen are based on my findings during a thirty-five year career working with managers at all levels. These represent a starting point for reshaping your career opportunities. Here is a quick look at the content you'll be viewing:

Part One: Where You Fit in the Organization (Chapters 1-5)
An aspiring manager needs a clear understanding of the organization's purpose (key performance indicators); how to structure the organization for effectiveness and efficiency; the key results expected from a manager's position; the multiple management roles and skills needed to succeed and the critical importance of personal credibility.

Part Two: Where Credible Managers Spend Their Time (Chapters 6-14)
There are key competencies that an aspiring manager needs to possess to drive organizational success and be noticed. Managers must have the knowledge and skills to create strategy, provide structure, install efficient processes, create the conditions for strong

human performance, manage human interactions, create a positive working climate, model sound operating values, and promote ongoing learning and manage change.

Part Three: Bonus Strategies that Accelerate Success (Chapters 15-20)

There are additional ways to leverage success on the path to advancement: finding a good mentor, managing your boss, mastering your 'mind thoughts', getting the best from consultants, managing cynicism and deciding if top management is really for you.

I sincerely hope the ideas in my book offers self-mentoring guidelines that help you.

Lawrence Anderson, Vancouver, Canada

CONTENTS

PART THREE

PART ONE

Where You Fit in the Organization

Chapters:

Chapter 1

The Purpose of Your Organization

Key Points for this Chapter:

1. *Start with a clear picture of the external results that represent real success for your specific organization and use them as the framework for business decisions and effort;*
2. *Establish the cause-and-effect relationship between the desired external results and the significant management functions that will achieve them;*
3. *Institutionalize the discipline of innovation to keep the organization renewed and flourishing.*

The higher you go, or hope to, in an organization, the more conceptual knowledge you will need, starting with the big picture of *why* your organization exists and *how* it can succeed and grow. Once this conceptual model is clear, your purpose in the organization becomes clearer. It helps you and others to appreciate how you each fit in the organizational setting and enables you to act in a purposeful way.

Each year, for as long as I can remember, *Fortune* magazine has published its annual report, "The Best Companies in America." To be chosen is great press and a mark of distinction. Whether you call them 'Best of Class' or use some other superlative, the pride that these companies must feel is unimaginable. Or, it could be one of "Canada's Top 50 Employers," another distinction worthy of note. Underlying such distinction is a successful organization and the public recognition must be incalculable in terms of image and, presumably, reward.

Private companies have the objective of creating and keeping customers and government organizations have the objective of providing cost-effective services that are needed and valued by their captive audience, the public. Economic downturns notwithstanding, there is a high correlation between organizational excellence and success. Years back, Peters and Waterman accelerated interest in the characteristics of successful companies with their classic book, *In Search of Excellence*. Even now, Jim Collin's books, *Good to Great* and *Built to Last,* reinforce interest in, and enthusiasm for, the secrets of organizational excellence.

For an Organizational Change Consultant (OCC) like me, these and other authors did us the favor of convincing senior managers that there were universal metrics and strategies to be used to measure and attain organizational excellence and that there are valid practices that need to be a part of a manager's makeup that help her or him to work *on* the organization and not just *in* it. This interest in organizational excellence has never ebbed. Nor will it. This is the ultimate challenge for all managers. *Creating a better organization increases in importance as managers move up the organizational ladder.*

Although I was a full-time OC sole-practitioner for thirty-five years and served many clients, I always found time to teach Organizational Behavior at local universities where I either lived or worked. Business students preparing for careers were naturally keen on learning the secrets of successful companies. Thus, when I began each semester, I asked them to ponder, discuss and agree on the answer to three basic questions:

1. Looking from the *outside-in*, what do excellent organizations achieve that makes them successful?
2. Looking *inside* these successful companies, what functions must they excel at to drive their external success?
3. How do these organizations continue to excel and grow?

In relatively short order, these bright and eager students typically arrived at opinions that looked similar to the findings shown in

Figure 1. These were fourth year students about to graduate. We then talked about the implication of their conclusions as it applied to their imminent entry into management. In the diagram, *Figure 1,* they quickly saw the cause-and-effect relationship between the organization's activities and the business results it achieves. Now, they had a context for the remainder of the syllabus: learning how each of the key management functions on the left-side of *Figure 1* are learned and performed. Questions 1 and 2, above, were answered in the exercise. Question 3 was answered intuitively: by enhancing existing products or services and by innovating and bringing new products to existing and new markets. Arriving at their conclusions through self-examination, their conclusions were practical and owned by them.

Figure 1: Organization Purpose: Cause and Effect

"CAUSES" Internally They Perform These Very Well	"EFFECT" To "Stakeholders" Successful Companies Look Like This:
1. They have a clear business **strategy**: (know their "market" and what they need to offer to capture customers)	1. Provide a **valued product/ service** to customers (quality, service, guarantees, warranty, etc.)
2. They have an effective **structure** that allocates responsibility and authority and enables communication	2. Are **profitable** and **financially sound** (balance of assets/ liabilities; positive cash flow; good credit)
3. They have sound **business processes and systems** that ensure efficiency	3. Are **growing** and have **longevity**
4. They have productive and satisfied **employees** who want to make a contribution	4. Are **honest** and **ethical** in their dealings with stakeholders; there is transparency of ownership
5. They have a positive **climate** and are considered a great place to work.	5. They comply with all **legal** requirements
6. Their **organization culture** promotes high standards for all conduct.	6. They contribute to the **community**, including the environment
	7. They are recognized as an **"industry leader"** (image, products, innovative, employer, etc.)

Johnson & Johnson regularly made the 'Top 100 Companies' in the annual *Fortune* magazine awards. Even though they recently had negative press because of product recalls in 2010 they typically exemplified the characteristics shown in *Figure 1.* They lived their published credo, or promise, and became a time-honored company. Now it is Apple or Microsoft or Amazon. Amazon started selling books on-line in 1995. Almost each year since, Amazon has used innovation to boost its success. In 2009 its colored E-reader kindle Dx was introduced with great success. Imagine at the time having access to the editorial content of major dailies each day, starting at 4:00am! Business media estimate sales of Kindle at $3.8 billion by 2012! I've read several articles extolling Amazon's virtues including how it focuses on selection, low price and product reliability. One of these countless articles described how Amazon starts with the customer in mind and works backwards from there to provide them with what they want. In my OC profession this is called "backwards thinking," a useful tool for first deciding what the customer wants and building organizational dimensions from there. Amazon's ongoing growth also appears to reply on innovation, just as *Figure 1* suggests. And what about Apple's I-Pod and I-Phone and I-What's-next? Innovation is part of a successful company's DNA.

Even in industries where costs are high and innovation isn't easy, some companies are able to distinguish themselves from the competition. A case in point: Canada's employee-owned domestic and spreading airline, WestJet. Originating in Western Canada as a local airline growing out of Pacific Western Airlines, WestJet has experienced remarkable growth at the expense of Air Canada, the country's premier carrier. The airline industry has suffered huge losses since 2000 caused by rising fuel and operating costs and less-than-full passenger loads. Competition is fierce; many airlines are in the red, Air Canada included. But not WestJet! It is profitable and growing. In 2009, seeking to differentiate itself from other carriers, primarily Air Canada, WestJet seized on a powerful marketing strategy called *Perkonomics.* The term, like perks at the office, meant added-value—at no extra cost! WestJet released its new (read innovative) Perkonomics in its widely-publicized 'Care-antee' as shown in *Figure 2.*

Figure 2 WestJet's 'Care-antee'

Not only was 'Care-antee' innovative, it was timely. In an article in Canada's *MacLean's* magazine, (October 2010) a *Time* equivalent in Canada, the lead-in to the article read: "WestJet's Plan to Crush Air Canada, the Country's Premier Airline". 'Care-antee' was innovative and bold. Air Canada was, and still is, in the red and losing more whereas WestJet is consistently profitable. 'Care-antee' was timely. It came at a time when North American and international airlines had all but removed free services and were now charging all kinds of add-on fees for on-board snacks, ear phones, etc., as well as on-ground services for reservations, seat selection and the dreaded changing of booked flights. Not WestJet. Check them on their website for the company history. Track their success. They epitomize the organizational characteristics the students noted in *Figure 1.* Not to take away from Air Canada. They were voted the 'Best Airline in North America' on a number of service-related metrics but they are unprofitable! And WestJet is gaining much more of the domestic market that Air Canada once dominated.

So, for *The Purpose of Your Organization,* the title of this chapter, I used *Figure 1* to focus on the big picture or strategic view that managers need to keep in mind. And, as a constant reminder, I urge them to retain a mental image of this picture as a reminder to work *on* and not just *in* their organizations.

Personal Exercise for Chapter 1

1. Spend time on *Figure 1*. Does it identify the main internal and external factors related to your organization's success? Create a similar chart, one that represents, in your best judgment, the right metrics for your organization's intended cause-and-effect variables. A single page should suffice.
2. Compare your organization's current performance against these metrics. Write down the improvements/changes this exercise prompts. Park them for now.
3. Look at the left-hand column in *Figure 1*. How well does your organization perform these key management functions? Do they apply to your organization's purpose? Are there other functions that you feel should be added to reflect your uniqueness? Can you see areas (causes) where greater skills are required? List them.

    Looking at your organization from this broad perspective is the starting point for getting ready to take on a top-down perspective, one that you'll need to move up in your organization, or up and out in someone else's

Chapter 2

How Your Organization Should Work

Key Points for this Chapter:

1. *Shift away from thinking only about your role and start working **on** your organization, not just in it;*
2. *Devote time to learning how your organization ticks; use the six universal elements that greatly influence an organization's effectiveness*
3. *Make adjustments, as necessary, to bring these organizational elements into a healthy balance.*

"Work *on* your business, not just in it." I can't remember where I read this quote, or who penned it, but it's worth repeating that managers need a sound conceptual knowledge of what makes an organization work! They must pay attention to the overall health of the organization itself and not just what their people and physical resources are achieving within their unit. Functional expertise is assumed, but organizational expertise is a bonus for aspiring managers.

To put this in context, here's a question I was once asked by my very best mentor: "If all your people were performing their jobs satisfactorily, what would your unique contribution look like . . . your added-value role?" I can say that it caused me to ponder for quite a while. So, if the answer doesn't come quickly to mind, this chapter is for you.

As an Organization Change Consultant (OCC) I have been asked many times what it is I do for a living and how one becomes an OCC. I use a medical metaphor to try to respond. When you go to a doctor for your bi-annual medical exam, you are subjected to a series of tests to determine your overall health: heart, lungs, bones, brain, eyes, ears, blood pressure, cholesterol, triglycerides, ear, nose, throat, colon and, depending on the basic findings, maybe even more tests. It's great to get a positive result but often there are a few areas you need to work on. For those, you get advice on what to do and maybe some prescriptions. That's what an OC consultant does only the patient is the client organization and the OCC is the 'doctor' who checks the vital signs that make a difference.

What are these vital signs? Look at *Figure 3.*

Figure 3: How Your Organization Works

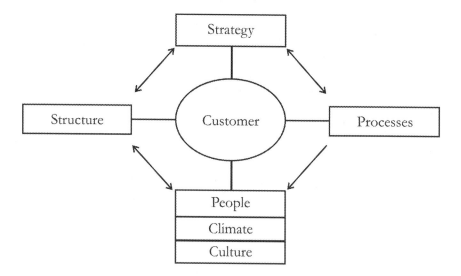

Organizational effectiveness, or, as I sometimes call it, 'organizational health', has been studied with results significant enough that managers can increase their knowledge of how organizations *should* work. Yet, it is mostly given a minor role in the curricula of university/college programs and then left to chance once employment begins. Each of the main elements in *Figure 3* is important for good organizational health but, as an interdependent system, it's clear that unless all elements are healthy, the negative effects of one or two can reduce the overall health of the rest. Think about the human body: high blood pressure, high cholesterol, gastro-intestinal ailments . . . all add stress and put a person's overall health at risk. Metaphorically, one or more of the main elements in *Figure 3* can do likewise to an organization.

So, the answer to the opening question is, simply: you work *on* your organization, not just *in* it. If you keep your organization healthy in all six elements, you experience peak performance. Try the following health test for your current organization as shown in *Figure 4*, using the elements from *Figure 3*.

Figure: 4 Organization Health Check

Patient (use you current organization)

Instructions: Using medical metaphors, give each criterion below a health rating using the following scale. (The higher the score the healthier the patient).

1. **Sick**: needs major prescription or intervention; maybe getting worse.
2. **Out of shape:** major conditioning needed to bring to acceptable level of health.
3. **Not serious**: Lots still working; areas needing improvement are being worked on with progress.
4. **Healthy on all indices**: keep up the good work. Take a bow. Live long.

Organization Health Checklist

Our Strategy *clearly* defines the market we're in, what products and services we'll provide and features high but attainable goals for the organization's performance. It shows how our goals will be achieved. Our people understand and support the overall organization goals and strategy.

Score: _____

Our Structure clearly defines who does what for whom and why. Responsibilities and accountabilities are clear and assigned to the right position. Accountability and decision-making are delegated as far down in the organization as possible. Work is organized and is coordinated vertically and horizontally without overlap or under lap. Job design enhances job satisfaction. We meet our functional goals.

Score: _____

Our Processes enable us to do our work with efficiency, with fewer resources, steps and less effort. We use systems that are targeted, friendly, timely, user-friendly and effective. These save time and cost.

Score: _____

Our People, all employees, are productive and satisfied, competent and committed; each is performing to standard or better. Conduct is business-like, teamwork thrives and conflicts are managed. Employee development is formalized; there is a succession plan in place for key positions.

Score: _____

Our Climate, defined as 'the workplace as perceived by all employees, not just their bosses', is given high-ratings indicating that it is a good to great place to work. Workplace conditions are such that people are enabled do their best and want to stay.

Score: _____

Our Culture clearly defines who we are: what we stand for and won't stand for. We have a recognized value system that defines high standards of conduct. We are ethical and honest in our business and employee relationships. There is a sense of pride that we are a responsible entity.

Score: _____

Our Customers, who really are #1, want to do business with us. Our products or services meet or exceed their needs. Given a choice of provider, they prefer us over our competitors. We enjoy repeat business, new customers, and excellent public image, good press . . . we're proud of who we are.

Score: _____

Give each element a score from **1** to **4** using the rating scale provided above. Do not average the scores because each element must be healthy in its own performance. For example, scores of 1 or 2 are obviously in need of a remedy now. Reflect on your assessment; ask others their opinions on these criteria. In later sections/chapters more information is provided on such remedies.

I have been using similar instruments with clients for thirty years. There is always some element of organizational performance that needs improvement in organizations, however big or small. I have been challenged by clients, usually senior management, with the argument, "How can we be expected to achieve a 4 rating in each element? That would be perfection! And, besides, how realistic is that in this competitive business, the economy and employee relations climate?" Fair enough. But, when I hear this, I hear the word 'rationalization' yelling in my ear. I want to use another medical metaphor and say, "I'm only your doctor; the test results came back and they are what they are. I can't take the pill for you . . . . that's your responsibility." But, I can't say that. Instead I might say, "You're right. Maybe perfection isn't likely in a complex organization; there are lots of variables working against it. But, getting the best possible organization performance is a suitable, alternative standard!"

Personal Exercise for Chapter 2

Your job as a manager includes keeping your unit, section, department, division, or whatever the correct title is, as healthy as your best efforts can make it. So, as you look at your ratings using the criteria in *Figure 4,* reflect and answer the following questions:

1. What are we doing that seems to be working okay and we should *continue as-is?*
2. What do we obviously need to *start* doing, or do more of, in order to improve?
3. What do we obviously need to *stop* doing, or do less of, in order to improve?

If you end up with a list of actions from this exercise, use it as your *organizational health strategy*. You will benefit from additional assessments of your unit by your Peers and employees providing the climate is trusting, open and honest. If it isn't, your own assessment will do for now. Remember, the elements in *Figure 4* are interdependent; a change in one or more will have an impact on the others. Until they are all working to the best of peoples' abilities, and working in sync, you're not quite done yet. So, the message in this chapter is: work *on* your organization, not just *in* it! That's how your organization should work!

Chapter 3

Your Job as a Manager

Key Points for this Chapter:

1. *Know the key responsibility areas of your position that will have the greatest impact on results;*
2. *Know the precise results expected of you in these areas that demonstrate you are meeting your responsibilities;*
3. *Implement the same rules with your employees.*

In the previous chapter, you were encouraged to begin working *on* your organization . . . not just *in* it. Once you know the broader picture shown in *Figures 1, 3* and *4* (go back and look at them as often as required), you know the context for your own responsibilities. In this chapter, you will personalize your own responsibilities more in line with what you are supposed to be achieving, only we'll go a little deeper because of its importance.

When I took my first management workshop as a new manager at Ford Motor Company with an internal company trainer who was exceptional, we were given the following definition of a manager.

> *A manager's job is the process of getting the right things done right through allocated physical, financial and human resources.*

We understood the notion behind the quote but wanted more specifics. As newcomers, we had a shared need to understand what a manager's job *really* was. But, as in most cases, we had to gain experience and make mistakes before the picture became clearer; not unlike Malcolm Gladwell's findings in *The Outliers*. Fast forward now to my first year as a management consultant with one of the former 'Big Eight' international firms: I was tagging along with my mentor, a senior partner, as a member of a team conducting a review of a government organization. We were interviewing department managers and a cross-section of employees (a must), soliciting input on the status of organizational health, similar to *Figure 4*'s criteria. My mentor kept his questions simple and to a minimum. For example, to gain insight into each manager's perceived understanding of his or her job, my partner would ask:

1. What are the Key Responsibility Areas (KRA's) of your management job?
2. How do you know whether or not you are doing a good job?

Most gave only general answers to the first question but few could really answer the second question. Imagine the potential loss of focus and efficiency that could arise from not knowing one's expected and measurable results! It might fly if the boss was happy with the status quo, even if for the wrong reasons which might include tolerating low standards; but it wouldn't fly with bosses whose expectations were far more demanding. Questions 1 and 2 are critical questions every manager should be able to answer.

The evaluation of human performance is not perfect and never has been because it is based on perception, which is not always objective reality. Thus, whatever can be done to mitigate subjectivity and perception error should be sought between employee and boss. One of my pre-consulting roles was as a trainer in the HR division of one of North America's largest auto manufacturers. A popular topic at that time was 'Management by Objectives', or MBO, also called 'Management-by-Measurement'. Thus, we approached the supervisors in our assembly plant with two requests:

• Tell us the Key Responsibility Areas (KRA's) for your job.

- Tell us the measurable results you need to achieve to be successful.

It was precisely at that time that I convinced the plant manager of the need for a new supervisory program. We kept promoting line workers to first-line supervision with next to no formalized training and watched as their life-expectancy diminished in the conflict-ridden assembly plant environment. We were given permission, formed a group of veteran supervisors and conducted a needs analysis of the new supervisor's job profile. Using the two questions above as a starting point, it took several back-and-forth meetings to arrive at a single-page, but meaningful, definition of the core dimensions of the job. Then, we produced several drafts to arrive at a description that looked like those in *Figure 5*, below.

Figure 5: Key Responsibilities of Production Supervisor

Key Areas of Responsibility		Measurable Results
AREA	DRIVER	EXPECTED RESULTS
1. Safety & Hygiene	Employee Health/Safety OSHA/Dept. Labor Responsible Employer	Clean work area; Zero lost time/No hazards/ Rules followed; First-aid capabilities
2. Production/ Customer Service	Profit Margins Customer Demands Reputation	Quantity & Quality per standard and production schedule
3. HR Management	Attract & Keep Good People	Hire good people who show up, can do their jobs, are cooperative, show initiative and enjoy work
4. Cost Control	Profit Margins Efficiency	Cost control evident; Finds ways to cut costs/no wastage
5. Equipment	Cost/Up Time	No improper use, well maintained, no breakdowns, repair backup/spares
6. Materials/Supplies	Product Quality	No wastage, no overstoring, supply J.I.T., No outages
7. Quality Control	Customer Satisfaction	Visual inspection; Zero defects
8. Records	Cost Control; Comparative Data to Measure Trends	Up-to-date, accurate payroll, inventory, aids dec-making, attendance

We tested the draft document in *Figure 5* with other bosses and could tell by their reactions that this approach had value beyond the supervisory program we were building. It applied to all jobs!

With approval of the supervisor's job profile, we then used our focus group to design the curriculum and learning experiences and find the instructors to lead the kickoff session. The result was a huge success: attrition eventually dropped, quality went up and employees responded favorably to a better quality of supervision. It took a while and wasn't perfect, but it was much better than in the past.

Examine *Figure 5* for a moment. It's not like the typical job descriptions you see, the ones written primarily for job evaluation purposes and not much else! These focus on lists of *duties* the incumbent performs in a job cycle. They try to show what the person does but omit the question, "For what purpose?" *Figure 5* tells the new supervisor what the *expected* results of the job are. This is the MBO approach mentioned at the beginning of the chapter. It makes sense and helps reduce perception error in performance evaluation because the results are measurable. Even the old quality gurus like Edwards Deming recognized that what gets measured gets done.

A quick comment on the value of the middle column called 'Driver'. Using it is optional, but I prefer it because it answers the question *why* each KRA is important. Give people a reason for what you ask them to do and, assuming it makes sense, cooperation goes up. It provides the sell.

How and where can a single-page document like *Figure 5* be used? The uses are many: recruiting, selection, orientation, performance feedback and improvement, remedial efforts and rewarding good results. Typical job descriptions don't enable these.

For managers wishing to work *on* their organizations, trying the KRA approach is a helpful strategy. KRA's will vary from job-to-job; each job has its own uniqueness and the drivers may be different. But the approach is valuable because every job can be defined in this manner. The end result is the ability to answer the questions, "What are your expected results?" and "How do you know if you're doing a good job?"

At one time I wrote an article on the use of MBO for defining a college teacher's job. My article was published in a monthly periodical of the *Ontario Institute for Studies in Education,* a part of the University of Toronto. The article showed my idea of the KRA's for a college teacher's position as shown in *Figure 6:* Faculty KRA's.

Figure 6: Faculty KRA's

KRA	DRIVER	MEASURE OF ACHIEVEMENT
1. Curriculum	Need for a current body of knowledge	Endorsed by a committee of external curriculum advisors
2. Learning Materials &	Utilize critical thinking and appeal to different learning styles	Evidence of multiple learning processes (cases, videos, projects and effective learning aids)
3. Classroom Facilitation & Management	Engage student attention and thinking; promote interaction	Full attendance; obvious participation; student evaluation of learning - teaching process
4. Student Counselling	No student failure attributable to learning process or lack of counselling	Students with learning problems diagnosed and helped
5. Records	Evaluation of learning and justification for grade	All required records completed accurately and on time, Ratings defensible
6. Self Development	Keep up with field of specialty and newer approaches for improved learning, staying current; enhancing value	Evidence of approved self study successfully undertaken

The article got mixed reviews. Academic Deans and Chairpersons liked the idea of KRA's for the evaluation of their teachers but the teacher's union didn't! We did not anticipate the politics of the situation. Collective bargaining was new to the players and, simply, the union would not support anything that they believed would be used negatively against a member. Their argument was weak: "We are professionals and, as such, professionals regulate themselves,"—a euphemism for 'back off'. But we were allowed to use the format for orienting and training new teachers . . . . the non-threatening uses. I found it sad, and still do, that formal performance evaluation is resisted in school settings when it is relatively easy to agree on the KRA's as suggested in *Figure 6* and to measure actual results against the intended results.

Personal Exercise for Chapter 3

Using the format in *Figures 5* and *6,* write the KRA's for your job on one page. Just list the areas first, like the left-hand column does. Limit the KRA's to 6 to 8. Then, focus on the 'significant few vs. the insignificant many' results that apply to each distinct area. It will take a few stabs at the exercise until you can look at it and say, "These *are* the most important areas where I need to get these results." Check it with your boss and peers. End with a one-page summary, no more, and document as shown in this chapter. Then, you can answer the two main questions at the beginning of this chapter:

1. Do you know the KRA's for your job i.e. expected results?
2. Do you know if you're doing a good job i.e. getting those results?

If this chapter makes sense to you, plan on creating a single-page summary of KRA's of all the positions reporting to you. Several may be doing similar jobs so, if one description covers several people, so much the better.

Chapter 4

Multiple Roles You Must Know How to Play

Key Points for this Chapter:

1. *Identify then master each of the key roles you will have to play to achieve your KRAs and expected results;*
2. *Start with an assessment of your current skill levels demanded by each key role;*
3. *Fill skill gaps with ongoing self-development and sponsored learning programs.*

Knowing your KRA's means the expectations regarding your job results should be clear. But to achieve those results will require you to play a number of different roles. And for each role you'll need to play, there are a host of skills that are part of it. Likewise, the roles and skills you'll need to play will depend on the situation you're in. In *Figure 5*, the new production supervisors understood *why* their position existed but did they know the roles that would be needed and were they skilled in those roles? Sound confusing? Not really. For missing skills, training would be required.

The best way I can explain this chapter is by borrowing from the work of Robert Quinn of the University of Michigan titled *Beyond Rational Management*. It is one of the most useful books I have read on the subject of managerial roles and has very practical implications.

I am showing one of Quinn's models in *Figure 7* to truly illustrate just how skilful and flexible a credible manager has to be.

Figure 7: Quinn's Multiple Roles of Managers

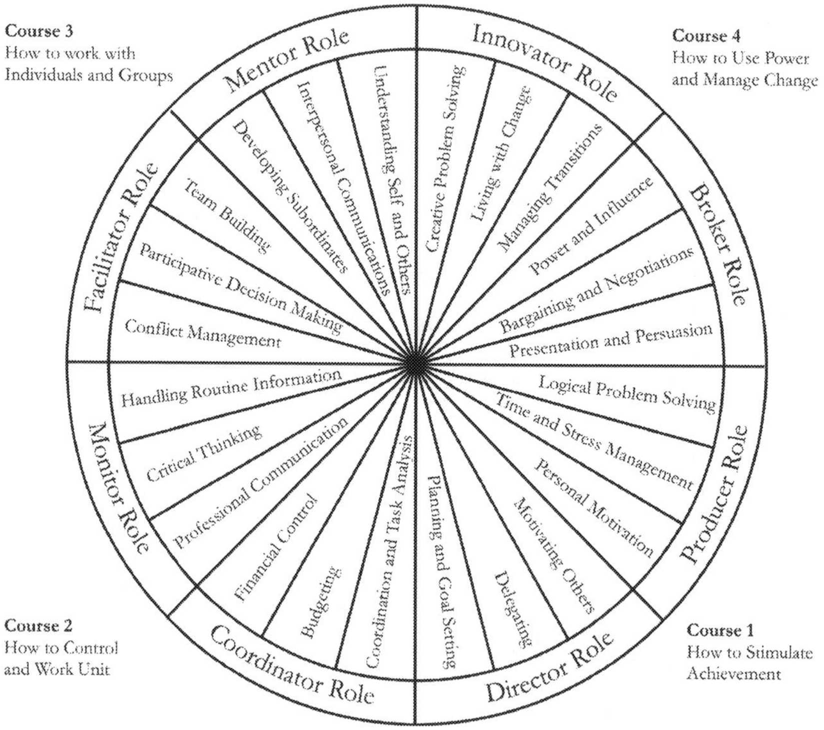

Course 3
How to work with
Individuals and Groups

Course 4
How to Use Power
and Manage Change

Course 2
How to Control
and Work Unit

Course 1
How to Stimulate
Achievement

According to *Figure 7,* managers play eight (8) distinct roles, each of which requires three (3) critical skills. There are more skills a manager needs than the model shows but the ones shown are primary thus it's not relevant to argue the point.

I have used Quinn's model to evaluate learning needs for managers as part of organization change assignments. It has been helpful, as well, to audit training/learning programs being offered as a means of making improvements. For every skill in the model there can be a learning opportunity. Managers can consult Quinn's model to assess their own development needs. In *Figure 8,* Quinn's approach for completing a self-analysis is provided. Resembling a bulls-eye target, each role is shown on a scale from 1 to 7, 7 being the optimum score. You can guesstimate your current capability for each by placing a dot on the spoke for each role. Some roles may be required more or less than others due to the nature of the job itself or the skills for a given role may be satisfactory or lacking. When you join the dots together on the spider's web, you immediately see your profile; where you're strong and where you need to develop. Examine the roles to which you assigned lower scores. Then look at the three skills that make up that role. Any gaps in your skills become your learning objective.

Figure 8: Self-Assessment: How are you playing your roles?

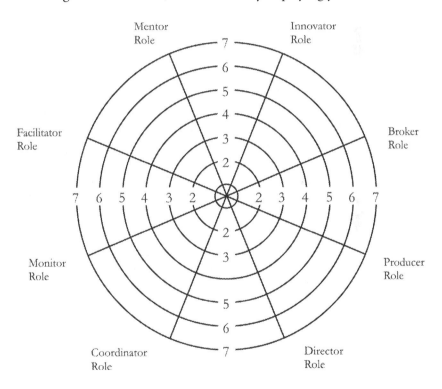

Sadly, not a lot of organizations provide adequate development for their managers. Business demands, time pressures and cost seem to work against in-house management development. It's expensive and the payers can't see an immediate payback. By default, most management development is self-development and that is often hit-and-miss. You will have to find your own opportunities for acquiring needed skills. Be on the lookout for workshops that offer applied skills, a.k.a. learning-by-doing. The most important skills I acquired on managing did not come from university classes or even on-the-job experience but from practical workshops loaded with simulations, role-plays, team-building, group decision-making, assertiveness training, facilitating meetings, pubic speaking and mentoring by inspirational role models. Building a sound personal library on management topics is also important, including works like Quinn's as illustrated in this chapter.

Personal Exercise for Chapter 4

Study Quinn's model and internalize the concept. Assess your current skill level in each of the eight roles and twenty-four skills using the bulls-eye diagram in *Figure 8* to record your ratings. Don't worry about being subjective. Next, list the skills you want to strengthen. Search for practical job assignments that involve these needed skills. Learn from colleagues who demonstrate a high-level of skill in the areas you want to develop. Do a topic search and seek materials on *how to* rather than just *what to* do to acquire a desired new skill. See what your organization has to offer in learning and development. Check out the local college offerings. Search for consultants who specialize in applied workshops. Subsequent chapters give tips on how to develop many of these skills. Google Quinn's work; there is a workbook that is especially good for diagnosing your current skill levels and prescribing learning remedies.

Chapter 5

What Having Credibility Means for You

Key Points for this Chapter:

1. *Your credibility comes from the perceptions and attitudes others have of you, not your own, and this makes your job easier or more difficult depending on how you 'come across' in the workplace;*
2. *Others' perceptions about your credibility influence their judgments on how they will relate to you;*
3. *There are definitions of 'managerial credibility' you can use to increase your self-awareness. Earnest self-improvement is a sign of maturity and increases your credibility not to mention your potential to advance.*

Credibility may be defined differently by people but you can be sure the adjectives used to define credibility are as plentiful as they are descriptive. Webster's says it means 'believable.' Ask yourself what 'believable' means and see how long a list you create. As part of the meaning, a good reputation is a significant part. See how far you can go in management without one!

We are guilty of judging others, but we do it anyway. Psychology blames our egos. We have this tendency to compare ourselves to others and judge them as the same, better or worse than us. Our attitudes influence our judgment and perish the thought that our egos will be bruised when we compare ourselves unfavorably to the behavior and image of others. Thus, my conclusion, after years in the OC/HR business, is: *all evaluation is subjective.* Perception is not always objective reality and perception errors mean that judgments are often unfair or wrong. Yet, we continue to judge others . . . and others judge us. We hope we convey a good reputation but do we? That rests on the perception others have of us . . . and the topic of this chapter.

Here's a favorite, and true, anecdote on credibility. One of the senior partners of the 'Big Eight' consulting firm I initially worked for was a master at cutting through to what he called, "the pith and substance of the matter." When, on an assignment, the client asked if a certain manager should be fired, I was ready to say, "Yes." I had conducted the departmental review and the results were dismal. However, my boss answered, "That depends." I have never forgotten what followed next and it taught me a valuable lesson. This is the exact dialogue where the client=C and my Boss=MB

C: "So, should I fire him, or not? What's your recommendation?"

MB: "Is he credible to his employees?"

C: "No."

MB: "Is he credible to his management peers?"

C: "No."

MB: "Is he credible to you; is he doing a good job?"

C: "Not really."

MB: "Is it costing you to keep him?"

C: "Yes."

MB: "So what do you think you should do in this situation?"

C: "Let him go."

MB: "We agree with your decision."

Years later, I still resort to this line of questioning when I am asked about terminating a client's employee. There was no way that my former partner was going to take the monkey off the client's back, thus allowing the client an 'out.' So, what is the point of the story? Too often organizations tolerate poor performance until they run out of choices and are forced to act. By that time, damage has already been done and everyone hopes that a new replacement will be a credible person. What they can't figure out is why this person remained on the payroll! The person being terminated operated without credibility; his or her reputation was a detriment to performance.

Managers are terminated every day in business. Their credibility is at the core of their dismissal. There are several reasons that account for it, i.e. they:

1. Were not meeting their KRA's. (Chapter 3)
2. Could not perform the multiple roles required of them. (Chapter 4)
3. Did not take heed of the drivers of their KRA's i.e. Why the job existed.
4. Could not conceptualize how the different parts of the organization interacted. (Chapter 2)
5. Could not gain cooperation from others, especially direct reports.
6. Had interpersonal behaviors that were offensive to others.
7. Showed a lack of self-awareness of their perceived credibility.
8. Consistently failed to meet expected standards of effectiveness and efficiency.
9. Failed to accept responsibility for substandard results and rationalized their poor performance.
10. Were unethical, unscrupulous or just plain dishonest.

On the other hand, credible managers have excellent qualities that their colleagues, bosses and employees can easily enumerate. Just think of the best bosses you've had and the point is made.

The perception as to whether a manager is, or is not, credible comes from others . . . not the manager. So, it doesn't matter how good you think you are unless this perception is shared. But some managers are blind to their weak spots; they lack self-awareness, an emotional intelligence (maturity) variable. Some insecure managers rationalize their weaknesses as caused by external events beyond their control. Blaming others or circumstances is part of their makeup.

Every year on National Bosses Day, good bosses get rave reviews and the bad ones don't. On Bad Bosses Day, quoted in several main dailies, these managers are now publicly acknowledged in worst-case stories, anonymously, of course, which are solicited and printed. Here is where you read such adjectives as bully, critic, saboteur, child, manipulator, and bosshole. The term, asshole, appears to be allowable now that it has been used in print by noted experts. The sad fact is that this appellation persists in the workplace even though it shouldn't. Although I can't bring myself to use the word (I consider it the ultimate put-down), I just had a flashback to the opening dialogue in this chapter between my partner and the client. I visualized the client calling in the manager and saying, "Sorry, but I have to fire you because everybody says you're an asshole!"

These kinds of managers exist in too many organizations, seemingly protected from harm, yet costing the organizations in terms of cooperation, effort and results. So, what to do? There are very good neutral benchmarks that can be used to assess a manager's credibility. The work of Daniel Goleman of Harvard on *emotional intelligence* is highly-persuasive and is a useful template for predicting the probable success of a manager. We intuitively know that credible managers possess both personal competencies and relationship competencies. Look at the summary in *Figure 9* from Goleman's excellent book, *Working with Emotional Intelligence.*

Figure 9: "Emotional Intelligence" Factors (Daniel Goleman)

PERSONAL COMPETENCE: These competencies determine how we manage ourselves	SOCIAL COMPETENCE: These competencies determine how we handle relationships
Self-Awareness = Knowing one's internal states, preferences, resources and intuitions • *Emotional Awareness:* Recognizing your emotions and their effects • *Accurate Self-Assessment:* Knowing your strengths and limits • *Self-confidence:* Having a strong sense of self-worth and capabilities **Self-Regulation = Managing your internal states, impulses and resources** • *Self-Control:* Keeping disruptive impulses in check • *Trustworthiness:* Maintaining standards of honesty and integrity • *Conscientiousness:* Taking responsibility for personal performance • *Adaptability:* Being flexible in handling change • *Innovation:* Being comfortable with novel ideas, approaches and new information **Motivation = the emotional tendencies that guide or facilitate reaching goals** • *Achievement drive:* Striving to improve or meet a standard of excellence. • *Commitment:* Aligning with the goals of the group or organization • *Initiative:* Ready to act on opportunities • *Optimism:* Persistence despite obstacles and setbacks	**Empathy = Being aware of others' feelings and concerns** • *Understanding Others:* Sensing others' feelings and perspectives and taking an active interest in their concerns. • *Developing /others:* Sensing others' development needs and bolstering their abilities • *Service Orientation:* Anticipating, recognizing and meeting customer needs. • *Leveraging Diversity:* Cultivating opportunities through different kinds of people. • *Political Awareness:* Reading a group's emotional currents and power relationships **Social Skills - Adeptness at inducing desirable responses in others** • *Influence:* Wielding effective tactics for persuasion • *Communication:* Listening openly and sending convincing messages

Goleman's findings came from third-party research and the data are considered empirically sound. That makes the characteristics on both dimensions of *Figure 9* useful for all manner of management development: for hiring, performance management, succession planning, improving work climate and, especially, self-development. Goleman's work has been a practical tool in my OC consulting as evident in the following three real cases from which a diagnosis of each person's emotional intelligence, or lack thereof, was made using Goleman's EQ model:

> **Case One:** The manager was a truly-gifted authority in his field. He used this as his single-source of influence or power. He showed impatience and irritability towards less knowledgeable staff, often resorting to public put-downs to force change. Staff turnover was high but he remained and so did the

toxic climate. One look at *Figure 9* helps confirm this client's unresolved problem; the manager's poor relationship management reinforced by a lack of self-awareness of his personal conduct.

Case Two: This manager valued friendly relations above all else and avoided any form of conflict. She preached teamwork, cooperation and civility. Up to a point this was good. But, by suppressing conflict, so were resolutions to pressing team issues. Tension remained in the section; several KRA's were below standard and remained static. Looking at *Figure 9*, where did she lack self-awareness and competence?

Case Three: The most senior employee was next in line for promotion. This person was disliked by co-workers for his overbearing puffery which they despised. They coped largely by ignoring him on a day-to-day basis. Sadly, the top boss decided to honor the established principle of promotion-by-seniority, saying, "He can learn about managing like I did . . . by being thrown into the fire." Isn't it obvious what abuse this senior employee will continue with added authority?

There are a lot of managers who just don't get it. As an OCC, I use a variety of diagnostic tools to get to the root causes of organizational problems, management appraisals included. Here is another bad example to serve as a good one, reminding those who hire managers to adhere seriously to established criteria, like Goleman's model, before making a final hiring decision. This was not the case in the three examples above.

Case Four: I was conducting an organizational review of the Finance Department of a national transportation company. The VP of Finance had been consulted about the review, which came down from headquarters, but was cool to my presence. Before my interviews commenced, I asked him if he wanted personal feedback if I received comments related to his leadership approach. "All right," he said, "but I wouldn't put too much stock in what you hear; these people have a history of bitching about everything." I reacted stoically to his opinion of his staff, knowing that I would meet many of these people in due course.

There were very few procedural roadblocks but the employees weren't very productive. Output was below expected standard. Some of the automated processes needed attention but my IT colleagues were on top of that. What came out in full-force, however, was the *climate* problem; "toxic" to put a word on it. The VP was described by staff as unpleasant and officious.

Staff, once given my promise of anonymity (but not confidentiality) as far as their information was concerned, dumped all over the VP. They claimed he was strict, harsh in his criticism, didn't suffer fools gladly, and was arrogant, rude and unfair. They suggested uncontrollable anger as a primary cause and mentioned that several formal grievances regarding his discipline were still in process between management and the union. In summary, this man was intensely disliked.

I record all interviews as close to verbatim as my quasi-shorthand allows. I do not add any interpretation nor analysis, just the remarks as passed to me willingly. When I approached him to give him the overall results of my review, he was quite buoyed by the relative absence of major process problems until, that is, I asked him if wanted to read the feedback about his style as offered by his employees. "Okay," he replied cautiously; "but, remember what I said about their continual bitching." I chose to forego an oral briefing and simply handed him a copy of the two-page litany of his alleged behavior and perceived character. He glanced at the first page and muttered, "I bet I know who said that." Then, as he read the remaining comments in silence, he finally said, "Anything else?" I suggested he reflect on the feedback for a few days at which time I would offer my opinions about possible resolutions.

For three days he did not report for work. When he did return, he initially refused to see me. As an OCC I felt I could not just drop the data in his lap and leave it un-discussed. Understanding was important. Besides, I had delicate information and he was not my client, his bosses were! In fairness, a meeting was essential. So, I persisted. I wanted him to challenge any errors-in-fact. The moment I saw him he immediately began opining. "When I read your remarks about me," he said, "I just got madder and madder. My reaction was anger and even revenge. I knew there were at least two employees I'd bring in for an interview. But that was before my wife got involved. When she asked me what was wrong, I handed her the list and told her what it was. Do you want to know what she said? She said, 'Yes, I see a lot of those characteristics in you . . . so do the kids'." He paused then said, "I trust my wife and that's why I am so upset. What can I do?" That was the beginning of a potential change in him.

On Goleman's chart in *Figure 9,* a key trait of a person with EQ is self-awareness. Why, otherwise, would a technically-qualified accountant behave so badly toward his staff? Why would he place his career, or even his continued employment, at such risk? Wouldn't persistent union and employee complaints tell him to check his behavior? Surely, he realized that the results of his behavior, over time, would not satisfy his needs for success and maybe promotion. What personal belief system was the basis for being so nasty? Did it give his ego a boost to lord it over others? Or, was he simply blind to his faults . . . or have a low EQ? This was a complex OC intervention and stands to illustrate the importance of EQ as a basis on which to hire and assess people in key executive roles. I don't know what happened to this young man or where he went after this employer. *Self-awareness*, therefore, is critical for managers to possess. And it is not easy! By adulthood, most people's behavior makes sense to them or they can rationalize it easily. But, as in the four cases presented in the chapter, each of the managers was blind to her or his weaknesses.

Another helpful tool that can be used to conduct periodic self-assessments to help correct deviant behavior is the Johari Window. The title is a combination of the two authors' names. A sample of the window is shown in *Figure 10;* it is another useful way to enhance self-awareness of one's personal behavior. Johari enables you to create the content in each of the windows as it applies to you. Examine this concept and try to see yourself in each of the windows. Of course, you'd need feedback from trusted sources to help you acknowledge your blind spots and to create a complete picture of yourself in the remaining windows. Self-analysis is a start.

Figure 10: Johari Window

	known to self	unknown to self
known to others	My Public Self	My Blind Spots
unknown to others	My Hidden Self	My Unconscious Self

Both the Goleman EQ chart in *Figure 9* and the Johari Window in *Figure 10* can be powerful aids to getting a better reading of your behavior and how you come across to others. More importantly, if the results of your behavior, over time, are not satisfying your basic needs, especially career mobility, something from these exercises should tell you what changes you need to make. A point to ponder:

what should the VP of Finance in case four see in the Johari exercise? Let's see:

Open Window: He knows he has strong technical skills, feels somewhat of an expert and has high expectations of himself and his direct reports. He does not, therefore, suffer fools gladly. He might feel he is a little too authoritative with staff on occasion but is rationalizing his behavior if he judges that staff does not share his work values. It is their lack of work ethic that makes productivity lower than it should be not, he believes, his values.

Blind Window: Blunt feedback is presenting him free information about how his behavior affects others. He can choose denial in the face of such inflammatory statements but the remarks are specific and negative and not easy to ignore when his wife agrees with them! Perhaps he will internalize these remarks and admit his misconduct and modify his behavior. One would hope so. Chances improve if this is the first time he can see the effects of his behavior on others and as a reason for lower employee productivity than attainable. But there is danger that he will rationalize his behavior by blaming others for his misfortune. That would be sad.

Hidden Window: Only he knows the underlying beliefs and attitudes that are driving his behavior. Maybe they are false assumptions and beliefs about others, about work ethic, about achieving perfection, about his self-importance, about distrust of others. Maybe it is deep-rooted cynicism or a lack of trust in others. Would these false notions account for his micromanagement? Could it stem from feelings of insecurity in dealing with others? What does it say about his EQ? He may need help in bringing his behaviors out in the open.

Unknown Window: Assume my report was going to be shared with the client, his bosses. What if they knew of his negative interpersonal behaviors? What if they weighed the competing values, i.e. productivity vs. employee satisfaction, and ignored the feedback? Nothing would happen! But, assume they want a positive and productive climate and were willing to give him confidential coaching by a third party. Assume they attached conditions to his coaching, i.e. a measurable improvement in the climate as perceived by the employees, within a short period. Would this type of intervention work? Maybe, maybe not; but it would certainly be worth a try.

Summing up this chapter, the credibility of a manager is one of the most significant factors in getting results with, and through, people. Tools such as Goleman's EQ and the Johari Window can lead to improved self-awareness. That's the prerequisite for behavioral change. Some managers are doomed to repeat counter-productive behavior and fail to reach higher levels of performance through better relationships. George Odiorne's warning, `things that do not change remain the same,` holds true for the cases described in this chapter.

Personal Exercise for Chapter 5

Use Goleman's EQ criteria and the Johari Window and rate yourself as follows: **1**=okay; **2**=needs attention; **3**=not okay. Show your self-ratings to people in your work setting you trust who know you and ask them to put their perceived numbers against yours. Listen to their reasons. Internalize their feedback. Make the final judgment yourself. Then, make three lists and monitor your behavior closely:

1. Behaviors I need to *start* doing, or do more of, and the payoffs for doing them;
2. Behaviors I need to *stop* doing, or do less of, and the payoffs for stopping them and;
3. Behaviors I should *continue* because they're working for me.

Part One, Where You Fit in the Organization (Chapters 1 to 5) is intended to provide a context for managers to help them appreciate their roles in the organization and the macro factors they must influence if they are to be seen as credible. In **Part Two, Where Credible Spend Their Time** (Chapters 6 to 14) the key competencies that drive organization performance, are illustrated.

PART TWO

Where Credible Managers Spend Their Time

Chapters:

Chapter 6

Creating Strategy

Key Points for this Chapter:

1. *Defining where your organization needs to go . . . that's strategic;*
2. *Master strategic planning and build understanding and support from the stakeholders as part of the process;*
3. *Manage implementation in ways that ensure the strategy is achieved.*

Strategy isn't limited to the intellectual exercise of deciding only the goals the organization must pursue; it includes the implementation of the strategy. Because of this important coupling, the overarching term 'strategic management' was coined. It is intellectually stimulating to attend the planning sessions, and a status factor if invited. Many managers go through the now familiar SWOT diagram exercise as shown in *Figure 11*, followed by writing mission statements, key performance indicators, goals, strategies and actions. Sometimes the planners go to offsite retreats where a facilitator leads the group through an agreed planning process. At last count, I facilitated about sixty such sessions working with the guiding members of the organization. The idea of offsite reflection and visioning is still a good business practice and an essential one.

But creating the plan is one thing; implementation, another. This raises the bar for promotion more than a notch because of the phenomenon known as the *knowing-doing gap.* Too often, when I was invited to update a client's plan a year or two after the first one, I initiated another SWOT exercise only to find that the previous year's SWOT was being duplicated! Not only were these SWOTs more-or-less the same, the strategic actions were also a repeat of the previous strategy meetings. So, the weakness of strategy-setting is not the thinking process that creates it, but the lack of planned actions that move the organization closer to its goals. This is universal weakness of strategic planning.

Mission Statements were usually part of the planning process. Some of these statements were pretty lofty. When I visited a client's premises, I always looked for evidence of a Mission Statement on the wall of the foyer or in company literature or in the boardroom. I began the practice of surreptitiously asking employees, "Can you tell me what the Mission Statement of your organization says?" Maybe you can guess the answer! Long before I offered myself as a facilitator of strategy-setting, I took a number of workshops on the subject and read about the approach to strategy used by familiar corporations. The notion of creating strategy finally hit home to me when I heard a facilitator say, 'The Apollo Eleven astronauts didn't aim at the moon for their first successful landing; they aimed where they expected the moon to be!'

Among the most successful strategies during one of the world oil crises in the 1970s was that of Royal Dutch Shell. Their scenario planning had a variety of strategies contingent on shifting scenarios, both possible and probable outcomes, and enough flexibility to shift direction quickly to the emerging scenario. But, for the average manager, there doesn't have to be a complex process for creating strategy. That's where this chapter is going, starting with the very useful SWOT process shown in *Figure 11*. "SWOT" is the acronym for Strengths, Weaknesses, Opportunities and Threats as these relate to the organization itself at a given time.

Figure 11: An Illustrative SWOT Diagram

INTERNAL ORGANIZATION	EXTERNAL ENVIRONMENT
Strengths 1. Capital 2. Product Experience 3. No Debt 4. Committed Stakeholders	**Opportunities** 1. Apparent Market Need 2. Can minimize risk 3. Can compete on uniqueness 4. Can compete on price/quality
Weakness 1. Inert Organization 2. Employed Turnover High 3. Aging Equipment 4. Not very automated 5. Physical Facilities	**Threats** 1. Two Strong Competitors 2. Possible Other New Entries 3. Government Regulation 4. Change in Economy 5. Consumer Loyalty to Current Providers

Assume that a group of ad hoc planners put their organization's SWOT together with, say, a limit of 5-6 key factors in each quadrant. Assume further that the facilitator has helped them rank the items in priority (a process for doing this is described at the end of the chapter). Once the SWOT is complete, several key questions apply:

1. How can we build on our current internal *strengths*?
2. How can we offset our internal *weaknesses*?
3. How can we leverage external *opportunities*?
4. How can we lessen, or offset, our external *threats*?

Answering these questions is the beginning of creating strategy, but not quite the end. Look at *Figure 11* again. This company has internal strengths to leverage success; but look particularly at the challenges under internal weaknesses. These are *organizational* by nature and there will have to be some major preparatory work done on the organization itself before being able to move toward any new goals. If you go back and glance at *Figure 3* in Chapter 2, you will note how interdependent the variables of strategy, structure, processes, people, climate and culture truly are. That's why working *on* the organization and not just *in* it is so important. I mention this to reiterate an earlier point: creating strategy includes successful implementation and you can imagine what will happen to a sound strategy if the organization gets in the way.

Let's focus on just the planning part, or deciding what the goals will be. This requires an open mind and the suspension of disbelief about the organization's future, or the exercise is pointless. When deciding strategy, I ask the client group to accept two *conditions*:

1. Theoretically, when planning, everything is possible; and
2. Operationally, there will be some hurdles but let's set that aside and plan without constraints.

A Case in Point: Edward Jones Financial Planners

When a small one-person office appeared in an off-main street location near my home in Vancouver, I wondered who Edward Jones was! The office was in a quiet area away from traffic and pedestrian flow. I knew they were USA-based, but little else. As I was thinking of examples to use in this chapter I came across a bit of their story in my *Harvard Business Review* file dated April, 2008. In *Figure 12*, this company's strategy is summarized. It is easy to comprehend; it says what it is trying to become and what it won't become. It describes its market or preferred investor, its products and its metrics for growth. Now that I am aware of how successful they have become, I notice more and more of their ads for financial advisors. Cool!

Figure 12: Jones Strategy Statement

Edward Jones's Strategy Statement

To grow to 17,000 financial advisers to 2012 by offering trusted and convenient face-to-face financial advice to conservation individual investors who delegate their financial decisions, through a national network of one-financial-adviser offices.

"conservative"

Our investment philosophy is long-term buy and hold. We do not sell penny stocks, commodities, or other high-risk instruments. As a result we do not serve day traders and see no need to offer online trading.

We charge commissions on trades because this is the cheapest way to buy stocks (compared with wrap fee, which charges annually as a percentage of assets) when the average length of time the investor holds the stock or mutual fund is over 10 years.

"individual"

We do not advise institutions or companies.

We do not segment according to wealth, age, or other demographics. The company will serve all customers that fit is conservative investment philosophy. Brokers will call on any and every potential customer. Stories about within Jones of millionaires who live in trailers - people all the other brokerages would never think of approaching.

"investors"

Our basic service is investment. We do not seek to offer services such as checking accounts for their own sake, but only as part of the management of a client's assets.

"who delegates their financial decisions"

We do not target self-directed do-it-yourselfers, who are comfortable making their own investment decisions. We are also unlikely to serve validators, who are merely looking for reassurance that their decisions are correct.

The above company strategy, as all should, answers three questions:

What/Who is our market?

What services/products will we offer?

What is our growth driver or how will we do this?)

Edward Jones passes the test admirably and has the success to prove it. The important message is that managers across the nation need to know how to craft such a strategy, engage support, get consensus and implement the plan. It doesn't matter whether you are creating your department's strategy or working on the corporate one; the process remains pretty much the same.

In terms of the planning process, it typically produces a hierarchy of company statements, also mentioned in the HBR article, as shown in *Figure 13* below.

Figure 13: Company Strategy Statements (HBR April 2008)

A Hierarchy of Company Statements

Organizational direction comes in several forms. The mission statement is your loftiest guiding light - and your least specific. As you work your way down the hierarchy, the statements become more concrete, practical and ultimately unique. No other company will have the same strategy statement, which defines your competitive advantage, or balanced scorecard, which tracks how you implement your particular strategy.

Mission
Why we exist

Values
What we believe in and how we will behave

Vision
What we want to be

The Basic Elements of a Strategy Statement

Strategy
What our competitive game plan will be

Balanced Scorecard
How we will monitor and implement that plan

Objective = Ends

Scope = Domain

Advantage = Means

These are the types of guiding words that communicate the organization's purpose and direction. If these metrics remain front-and-centre and are tracked and measured and announced, chances of successful implementation increase. Creating these documents is the role of top management. Defining the purpose and direction of the organization begins the process of strategic management.

Personal Exercise for Chapter 6

There should be adequate information in this chapter to let you try a practice hand at creating a strategy for your present organization be it a section, department or larger enterprise.

1. Create a SWOT diagram for your unit using the example in the chapter as a guide.

2. Limit yourself to 5-6 items per quadrant. You may find you have more to begin with.
3. List the suggested actions that flow from each of the listed items.
4. Use the Edward Jones example to write a similar statement for your unit. Call it a draft.
5. Engage others in your unit who are affected by an updated strategy. Co-opt their support.
6. Once you get consensus, publish the strategy and track and report progress regularly.

Method for Ranking SWOT Items:

Use the following directions in *Figure 14* to help you put your quadrant items in priority order. Examples are shown for internal strengths and weaknesses only; follow the same calculations for external opportunities and threats. This will place your items in order of priority so that your actions cover the most important ones.

Figure 14: Calculating Strength of SWOT Forces

Method for Ranking SWOT Items

Instructions:

1. List your top 5 Strengths below in column 1.
2. In column 2, give each strength a score from 1-10 based on how sure you are each strength is proven (10 is high)
3. In column 3, use the same 1-10 rating scale to assess the impact of the strength, i.e. the extent to which it makes a significant difference in performance outputs.
4. Multiply columns 1 and 2 to define the relative "Power" of your top 5 strengths. The highest score in rank order 1.

List Strengths	"Am I Sure?" PROVEN	"So What?" X SCOPE	=POWER	RANK

Internal Weakness Evaluation (Follow the same process as for strengths)

List Weaknesses	"Am I Sure?" PROVEN	"So What?" X SCOPE	=POWER	RANK

Chapter 7

Providing Structure

Key Points for this Chapter:

1. *Understand the distinction between effectiveness and efficiency as a rule-of-thumb for assessing the soundness of your current structure;*
2. *Structure jobs in a way that ensures effectiveness and efficiency on an individual level and build-in intrinsic motivating job content in the process;*
3. *Make sure everyone knows 'who' reports to 'whom' for 'what' and 'why' and is held accountable.*

Structure follows strategy, or so the literature says. It makes sense: a new strategy increases the chances that some structural change may be necessary to implement the new plan. But, you don't have to have a new strategy before working on your structure. That can happen any time. A simple way to look at the adequacy of your current structure is to ask, "Does our structure enable both effectiveness and efficiency for our organizational purpose?" If it does, you're doing the right things, right. But, it's important to make sure the distinct terms—effectiveness and efficiency—are understood and are being optimized. Not everyone understands the difference. I use to remind students of this distinction with a helpful anecdote I took away from one of the many workshops I enjoyed.

An elderly lady calls the local newspaper to place an ad in the obituary column for her recently-deceased husband. She gets the Obit sales clerk on the line.

Lady: "I'd like to place an Ad. My husband of fifty years has died.

Clerk: "I am so sorry. What would you like it to say?"

Lady: "How about, 'John MacDougal died.'"

Clerk: "Is that all?"

Lady: "I can't afford any more."

Clerk: "Well that would be effective all right; it'll do a basic job. But we can give you seven words for the price of three; that would be more efficient . . . provide more for the same, wouldn't it?

Lady: "More for the same? Yes that is a better deal, thank you."

Next day the ad read: "John MacDougal died; golf clubs for sale."

Before tinkering with the structure and changing roles and reporting relationships, a good rule-of-thumb is to answer two questions:

1. Are we achieving our product/service quality and delivery goals consistently? If we are, we're *effective.*
2. Are we doing all that with minimum resources i.e. less time, fewer people, less material, full machine time, lower cost, reduced effort, less waste, etc?. If we are, that's *efficiency!*

   If the answer to these questions is positive then, organizationally, your structure may be fine . . . so far. But, digging deeper, there are further cascading questions to consider, i.e.
3. Is it clear who reports to whom for what?
4. Is each person producing results that are both effective and efficient?

5. Are we coordinated horizontally i.e. across departments, and vertically, between hierarchical levels.

A Case in Point: The Poor Handoffs

A company making customized heavy machinery for a specific industry encountered a horizontal coordination problem because of its functional organization structure. Each specialty department was working in silos. Here's how it looked at the time of the incident:

- Sales Engineers sold the product
- Engineering at home office designed the application
- Manufacturing fabricated the product in the main factory
- Installation specialists assembled and tested the product on the customer's site
- Sales Engineers provided customer follow up during the break-in/warranty period

One product, huge in size and very costly, took months to produce. Delays caused extra overtime to meet schedule and the cost of moving the product on a flatbed truck was underestimated. When the product finally arrived and installation began, the enormous product didn't fit its housing on the customer's property! It was returned to the factory, re-fabricated, returned to the client . . . and installed a second time. This was a financial loss to the supplier, not to mention harm to its reputation. Immediately, there was finger-pointing among and between the departments that had touched the order.

The *silo* structure was at the root of the problem. Functional structures require cooperation and coordination, not to mention fail-safe, hand-off processes. The supplier's structure failed the tests of effectiveness and efficiency. There's an old saying I remember: "when everyone's responsible, no one's responsible." Everyone blamed someone else; no one accepted responsibility for this fiasco until the CEO stepped up and sought input on a structural/process solution. In the end, a cross-functional team made up of one key member of each department managed all future orders, as a group, from beginning to end. This team became responsible for future orders, and it worked.

Another key aspect of providing structure is *job design:* defining the responsibilities and tasks of individual jobs. Back in the 1900's, Frederick Winslow Taylor introduced the engineering approach to job design by measuring the amount of work a trained employee could complete in a designated time. I remember the presence of a large staff of industrial engineers when I began in HR at Westinghouse. There were twenty or so product divisions in the company at that time and these engineers set the work standards for each operation with their ubiquitous stopwatches.

When I joined Ford Motor Company, both Process and Industrial Engineers were plentiful. They designed each step of the assembly-line process and set the standard times for completion of each production/assembly cycle. Henry Ford is given credit for perfecting the assembly line. It was all about efficiency, doing the job in the minimum time with the least effort and the least number of steps and workers. This was efficient, or could have been, until the arrival of the human relations movement sometime in the 1970's. Of course, the unions would argue that they forced the passing of the Time and Motion Era.

In the 1970's, there began a shift to the psychological approach, i.e. the emphasis on designing individual jobs for intrinsic value, or motivation, as it was thought. In Organizational Behavior (OB) courses, the work on job design by Hackman and Oldham (Google for details) examined ways to enrich jobs. By understanding the key factors that provide intrinsic satisfaction to the job holder, it could mean greater productivity and lead to a more-satisfied job-holder. This is important. What a manager delegates to an employee has the potential of making the work and the employee response more positive. So, it became a case of what to add or take-away from the job content to reach this mutual goal. Does job design work? Can it lead to greater individual effectiveness and efficiency?

Hackman and Oldham identified five (5) key dimensions of a job that contribute to increased interest and effort. Jobs designed with these dimensions, which may require tinkering with job duties to achieve, could lead to improved interest, effort and satisfaction. Here are their five dimensions:

1. **Job Variety:** assigning a variety of duties involving the use of several skills
2. **Task Identity:** the employee can see where the job fits into the whole operation
3. **Task Significance:** there is a sense of the importance of the task
4. **Autonomy:** the employee is given latitude to decide how the work is done
5. **Feedback:** the employee can see for her/himself how well the job is being performed.

This is a potentially powerful tool for increasing employee productivity and satisfaction . . . if you use it! If you periodically look for ways to increase the intrinsic interest in any job reporting to you, consider the five dimensions described above.

Think about yourself for a moment. As a manager, are there tasks that you have long mastered that are routine for you but you still keep? If you delegated some of these to your subordinates, is it possible they would find the new duties interesting or challenging? Are there tasks that your boss is routinely performing which, if given to you, would add to your satisfaction and interest, not to mention giving you new skills that will help you to move up? To sum up, providing structure (this chapter's heading) also includes individual job design. If it can motivate your people, spend time looking at each job you oversee.

The term 'accountability' also falls under providing structure, i.e. 'who' reports 'whom' for 'what' and 'why'! The larger the organization, the more complex it gets. There is a need to clearly define responsibility and authority for each job holder. A simple way to clarify accountability is through a pictogram called RACI, an acronym representing:

R = is the person or function with the primary **responsibility** for performing the task;

A = the person or function with the **authority** to make the final decision for the task, including approval or veto;

C = defines who must be **consulted** before any final decision is made;

I = defines who must be **informed (c.c.d)** when the decision is made.

These terms lend themselves nicely to chart form. Once published, there is no confusion about who is accountable for what. Below is a RACI pictogram involving the current responsibilities of a client's Customer Service Department where neither effectiveness nor efficiency was being achieved. See why.

Figure 15: RACI Chart (Former Structure)

EMPLOYEE/POSITIONS

TASKS/JOBS	A	B	C	D	E	F
1. Order Receipt	R					
2. Inventory List	I	R				
3. Parts Ordering		I	R			
4. Bundling Orders			I	R		
5. Shipping				I	R	
6. Customer Expediting					I	R
7. Warranty Claims	R					I

In many hierarchical and functional organizations, the picture in *Figure 15* would not be uncommon. As shown, each employee (A through F) has a piece of the customer order but no more. It's a case of, 'I give it to you; you give it to her, she gives it to . . . . ' This is specialization at its peak. There are two noticeable gaps here: (1) there is no attempt to enrich the jobs using the five dimensions of Hackman and Oldham and (2) none of the six employees has an A . . . the authority to make final decisions! Has the manager kept all the A's?

If the manager tinkers with the jobs and wishes to push decision-making as far down as possible, here's what the new RACI chart could look like a few months later, after the manager changed delegation practices while adding any needed training:

Figure 16: Revised RACI

EMPLOYEE/POSITIONS

TASKS/JOBS	A	B	C	D	E	F
1. Order Receipt	RA			RA		
2. Inventory List	RA			RA		
3. Parts Ordering	RA	I		RA	I	
4. Bundling Orders		RA		RA		
5. Shipping	I	RA	I	I	RA	I
6. Customer Expediting			RA			RA
7. Warranty Claims	I		RA	I		RA

Look at the before and after RACI charts. What's the difference? Through job design, the jobs have changed and feature more potential motivating forces than before. Compare the contrasting results shown in *Figure 17*.

Figure 17 Hackman and Oldham

Job Dimensions	OLD (FIGURE)	NEW (FIGURE)
(Variety)	Each person has one function	Each person has several functions
(Identity)	Limited to one job	More parts of the whole process
(Significance)	Limited importance (one task)	Increased importance: several parts of the process
(Autonomy)	Limited: no authority	Increased autonomy: can make final decisions
(Feedback)	Limited once task finished	Increased with multiple functions: sees more impact of results

Through revising job content, a part of structuring, and giving experienced employees the A, or authority, to make decisions on their own, there will more than likely be improved section effectiveness and efficiency with more inherent job interest. In RACI, the objective is to push the A as far down as possible . . . to the job holder. That is what accountability is all about.

A final caution on providing structure: as organizations grow in size and complexity, finding effective and efficient systems for keeping the right information flowing to the right people on time gets harder. The exponential growth in the number of interactions between and among people in a growing organization can cause chaos. Intranets, i.e. e-mail, voice-mail, texting, all have a use. But, for communications that have an emotional content or involve potential conflict, only face-to-face communication works (more on that in the HR section).

Personal Exercise for Chapter 7

Apply the definitions of *effectiveness* and *efficiency* from this chapter to all functions of your department. Are there areas where you need to improve?

Look at your horizontal relationships with other departments or sections. Are there improvements needed in *coordination* and *cooperation?* Can essential handoffs be made smoother?

Look at each job holder. Examine each against Hackman and Oldham's five dimensions as illustrated in this chapter. Can you see how changes in your delegation habits can improve the intrinsic motivation of the employees?

Are you pushing the A—the authority to decide—as far down to the employees as possible to increase responsibility and accountability?

Chapter 8

Use Processes that Drive Efficiency

Key Points for this Chapter:

1. *Examine current processes for effectiveness and efficiency; engage employees to help;*
2. *Make improvements to existing systems and procedures and continually monitor results;*
3. *Stop using inefficient legacy processes, opting for improved ones.*

Processes are usually a sub-category of structure, which was discussed in the last chapter. Managers engage in structure when they define responsibility and authority and when they construct job content. They are also structuring the way work is done when they design and install proven systems that enable efficiency. How a job is done is a major enabler of effectiveness and efficiency because it serves to save time, effort, cost, use of materials and prescribe standards of quality. How work is performed is so important that a review of current practices should occur regularly.

'Best practices' is a term that became popular during the renewed quality movement in the manufacturing sector when offshore competition, especially in the electronic and auto industries, challenged domestic markets. At its core, the objective is to achieve optimum efficiency by removing the non-value-added steps in a cycle of a job process. There are so many automated systems, upgraded almost daily, used today that it is hard to keep up with the changes. Few manual systems remain. Almost every function from Sales and Marketing, HR, Operations, Logistics, not to mention personal efficiency applications, relies on automation. I cannot offer a current opinion on which, of many automated systems, works best and leave that to technical/functional experts. Suffice to say that a forward-thinking manager has to stay current in terms of new ways to achieve efficiency.

What I will offer are a few cautions for consideration when contemplating a change in any system:

- Tempting as they are, automated systems, especially enterprise systems, have hidden costs among which is the time it takes to manage the human condition, a.k.a. introducing and building support for change and mitigating employee resistance, the bane of implementation. Getting people to 'let go' of imbedded systems requires education, co-opting of opinion leaders, training and the celebrations and rewards for successful implementation.
- Implementation usually takes longer than supposed and even longer until the human condition is managed.
- Automated systems often change job content requiring possible changes in pay systems.
- The term 'user friendly' comes to mind as another of the criteria used to choose new systems.
- False starts often follow when a department switches to a new system.
- Horizontal handoffs are, at times, hindered until and unless departments that rely on coordination of effort are all on compatible systems.
- It takes guts to admit that a new system doesn't work. The sooner that happens the better.

So, even though you may have to rely on the systems people, it behooves you to remain mindful of the above cautions when planning systems changes.

Personal Exercise for Chapter 8

Try forming a systems improvement team among your employees. After selling the importance of efficiency, focus the discussion on the following question: "What changes and improvements for the better can we suggest that will make us more effective and efficient and ensure we still have fun?" This usually does lead to agreed improvements.

Chapter 9

Managing Others to Want to Do Their Best

Key Points for this Chapter:

1. *Before expecting to be successful at managing others, manage your own behavior first and last;*
2. *Internalize the main functions of the Human Resource Development process;*
3. *Master these HRD practices to optimize human performance.*

Managing others is a *conditional* skill. It's all about influencing others to want to do what you want them to do and do it to the best of their ability. I remember my first management course where I, along with other new managers, sat with great anticipation as the facilitator began the session on managing others.

"What's the first thing to remember when managing others?," he asked. There was a chorus of opinions all directed at the employees: their satisfaction, concerns, skills, needs, ambitions, behavior . . . the list was long. And then he said, "The first thing to remember is: manage your own behavior at all times; you have to earn respect." That still proves to be sound advice before digging into this chapter which is longer than most given its importance and my bias.

On more than a few corporate HR and corporate strategic plans, you'll find the phrase 'Attract, Develop and Retain Good People.' Who can argue with that intent? But, when you consider the differences in people's values, attitudes and patterns of acquired behavior, the above strategic statement is a great challenge. How good are you at attracting people through recruiting and selection? How skilful are you at developing people? And do you know how to create the kind of workplace climate that would make people want to stay and do their best? This is the ultimate challenge for managers seeking upward mobility.

When Ford Motor Company almost went bankrupt in the late 1970's early 80's, they were saved, in part, by 'Team Taurus'—a new way of working that emphasized employee involvement and union cooperation. The Taurus sold a record number of units and garnered many awards for excellence. I recall the Chairman at the time saying, "Its success was fifteen percent technological and eighty-five percent employee relations." As a former Ford employee in labor relations and HR, and now an external OC consultant, it's true that I tend to see people at the core of most organizational solutions. I recall Henry Mintzberg of McGill University claiming in one of his studies that the successful managers he found spent roughly forty percent of their time interacting with their people. Doing what, you may ask! One look at the Human Resource Development Process in *Figure 18* shows you *where* and *why* a good manager spends time with others.

Figure 18
Human Resource Development Process

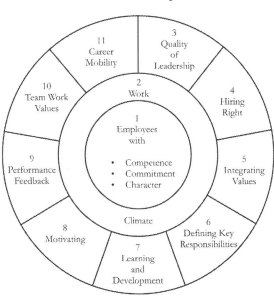

Figure 18 is a holistic model-at-a-glance representing the key HR responsibilities of a credible manager. Each of the separate HR competencies has its purpose but they act interdependently to produce top quality people. If you want top quality people, you need a depth of skills in each of these HR functions. Here's a synopsis of the key elements by its corresponding number in the diagram:

1. **The employee is the centre of attention.** Managers who don't get this pay an awful price. Remember the VP of Finance in Chapter 5? Unlike inanimate resources, people in a work setting make up their own minds about how hard they will work at what they do and the extent to which they will or won't support the organization's mission and goals. For attaining optimum employee support and effort, attracting and developing employees with Ken Blanchard's (of Situational Leadership fame) two C's: *competence* and *commitment* to do the job is essential. A third C, *character* is also critical and may be subsumed in the SLT theory.

2. **Work Climate** is best defined as 'the workplace as perceived by those who work there and not their bosses.' Thus, the conditions and policies under which people work affect their attitudes and behaviors. Dissatisfaction with workplace conditions suppresses productivity and employee satisfaction. Having a great place to work has been shown to be a major factor in attracting, developing and retaining good people. (Google 'Great Places to Work' for definitions of "work climate.").

3. **Quality of Leadership** is where the credible manager enters the HR process. In Chapter 5, *Figure 9*, the qualities of a manager with EQ were described. Thus, to make human resource development work best, the manager must have the personal qualities to be able to influence others to want to do their best. You could say that the quality of leadership is what makes the rest of the model in *Figure 18* work!

4. **Hiring Right** is where the HRD process starts. Hiring right means you have verified each new hire's competence, commitment and character. Skill in interviewing is expected and easily learned but, more importantly, reference-checking with past employers, not personal references, is an absolute must before any offer is made. Horror stories abound because of situations where references were skipped because the candidate looked good or the pressure to fill a job was significant. Interviewing skills are core skills for all managers . . . not just for hiring, but for everyday interaction, as in, "How's it going?" or "What's happening?" or any situation where 'what', 'how', 'who', 'when', 'why' or 'where' is needed for eliciting useful information.

5. **Integrating Values** is where you find out what's important to the employees, i.e. their values as it relates to their work and career expectations, and introduce them to the organization's core values. The latter needn't be sophisticated as long as it's clear. I had a boss who explained his expectations and values like this: "Show up every day on time, do your assigned work to the quality required, honor teamwork and cooperation, tell me if the flow of work is in jeopardy, offer constructive ideas to improve the status quo, support company goals

and values . . . and have fun. Clear enough?" This is a good time to ask for and record employees' personal goals i.e. their definition of job satisfaction including preferences for work-life balance.

6. **Defining Key Responsibilities (KRA's)** was previously described in Chapter 3, *Figure 5,* with the KRA's of the sample supervisor. That is what is meant here. Having a single-page document of the approved KRA's of each job has many benefits. It can serve to aid hiring, training, performance feedback, rewarding, promoting and, yes, firing. This type of document is a great discussion starter for confirming responsibilities and giving feedback on performance at any time.

7. **Learning and Development** (it's okay to call it training) starts at step 5 of the HRD model. Learning intensifies during one's break-in and continues informally and formally. Credible managers create and use an Individualized Development Plan (IDP) for each employee showing completed learning and remaining learning gaps. The KRA's should the focus of learning; they define the skills that are needed. This is also where development plans are agreed, both organization-delivered and the employee's own self-development. **Caution:** too many managers believe they are effective trainers when they are not! I like the old saw; 'If the learner hasn't learned, the trainer hasn't taught.'

8. **Motivating Employees** The question 'how to' motivate people is one of the most-asked questions I hear as an OC consultant. In this morning's paper the Sally Forth cartoon seemed apt when she says to her husband, "My staff doesn't do anything I say. They just don't respect me at all!" He replies, "Maybe it's time to get a new staff . . . fire the lot of them. Burn the deadwood and move on." In the last panel he closes with, "If I ever get a staff they're gonna live in fear." This challenge is sticky for many managers, so I have devoted a subsequent chapter to this key HR capability.

9. **Performance Feedback,** a.k.a. performance management and/or performance appraisal, is another critical capability that credible managers possess. Done well, it reinforces

employee motivation and preserves the employee-manager relationship. But, done poorly . . . . ! Having a document like the KRA sheet to use as the neutral criteria of evaluation takes a lot of subjectivity out of the evaluation. In this model, it's important to note that performance feedback is *not* the annual performance review. Those don't really work because they deal in the past. It is feedback that happens at any time, for whatever reason, whenever it's needed. Its purpose is to reinforce good behavior and extinguish unacceptable behavior. It avoids unpleasant surprises at annual review time. Imagine that one of your KRA's is to make your people winners. Each interaction, therefore, is important in keeping expectations whole. **Note:** If you do have an annual performance appraisal process as part of policy, try having the employee complete and present a self-evaluation to be used as the basis for discussion. When my mentor did this to me the first time, it was incredibly effective.

10. **Teamwork Values** are those you can see when employees respect and get along with each other. When it's working, you see cooperation, information and task-sharing, conflict resolution, empathy and mutual respect. This is another key element of a good human resource development process.

11. **Career Mobility** is especially relevant for employees whose personal interests are leading them to more responsibility, recognition and advancement. Not everyone wants that; some are content where they are in their careers. The credible manager knows the interests of each employee and tries to provide development opportunities for their interests to be realized. Otherwise, retention becomes a problem for the aspiring and upwardly mobile employees who do not see opportunities they seek. Each employee's IDP, mentioned at step 5 above, should be the basis for planned/approved development and for succession planning. People who are *immediately qualified* for the next level are IQ's while those who need *more experience* are called ME's.

To sum up, a credible manager sees the immediate value and interdependent nature of the HRD processes in *Figure 18,* and realizes that each of these HR processes needs to be healthy in its own right. When combined, they contribute to a positive HR climate that shows respect for stakeholders and enables them to succeed.

A word about HR departments: If you have one, the HRD process described in this chapter may be one of their functional specialties. You should embrace them as valued partners and use their expertise. **Caution:** At the end of the day, however, you are responsible for the conduct and success of your people . . . not the HR staff.

Personal Exercise Chapter 9

Spend time viewing and internalizing the various parts of the HRD process in *Figure 18.* Look carefully at each element and rate how effectively each is being performed by you at this time. Are you skilled in each function or do you need development? This becomes your HR Individualized Development Plan (IDP). In this chapter I described what a credible manager needs to understand to get the best out of the HRD process. In Chapter 10, some of the most common HR challenges will be amplified in terms of *how* these can be done.

Chapter 10

Human Performance Challenges

Key Points for this Chapter:

1. *What motivates individuals depends on their values, not yours! This is the secret to motivating your people and getting cooperation from others;*
2. *Pay attention to the quality of your relationship with each employee, peer and superior;*
3. *Be assertive in dealing with each individual's performance and use feedback, often, to get the behavior you want.*

When it comes to the subject of managing people and relationships, too many managers pass it off as 'common sense' or 'intuition.' These managers believe they are good with people yet anonymous surveys in my line of work often show the opposite. Simply, many managers are not successful in influencing their people to *want* to do their best. At least Sally Forth, the new manager mentioned in the last chapter, admits she doesn't know how to get cooperation. There are, to emphasize the point, quite a few boss-holes out there relying on their title to get compliance, yet they remain convinced they don't need people skills. Managers with high EQ's don't fall into the latter category.

In the previous chapter, *Managing Others to Want to Do Their Best*, I described the basic HR functions a credible manager needs to master. In this chapter, I want to answer questions that I have been asked repeatedly by client managers and university students. Here are the key questions:

1. What's the best way to motivate people?
2. How much time should I spend with my people because I'm busy too?
3. How do I deal with poor performers?
4. How do I manage difficult people?

I'll answer these important questions with anecdotes and prescriptions. Try to imagine how you, as the manager, might fit into each scenario and apply it in your own situation.

The employee makes the ultimate decision whether or not to give you the performance you want and have a right to expect. But you can exert influence by using both your title and interpersonal power and usually prevail in getting what you want . . . . if you are seen as *credible*. The key is in understanding each employee's basic expectations or values. Individuals have basic needs at work, for example, 'to achieve satisfaction and avoid dissatisfaction' (using Frederick Hertzberg's Hygiene Theory of Motivation). People value a lot of things in a workplace but they also place little or no value on other things. So, what some want others don't and vice-versa. Here's a case where values played a big role in achieving mutual satisfaction and motivation.

A skilled and highly-respected management consultant in a large, name firm was acknowledged by peers as partner material. Clients loved her and so did the junior consultants she supervised. At a late afternoon meeting of the partners on a Friday, a decision was approved to offer her the coveted partnership status that they assumed all aspiring consultants desired. Universalizing their feelings about the value of partnership to *everyone*, they chose to publish the announcement of her promotion on the company intranet. On the following Monday morning, after receiving a host of spontaneous smiles and words of congratulations, she walked into the managing partner's office, obviously embarrassed, and declined the promotion! Who would turn down such a prestigious vote of confidence? That's what all the partners were asking themselves.

Herein lies the first rule of motivation: Do not assume what is important to you is important to another! Here's a great quote I got from one of Chuck Dwyer's videos. He is a professor from the Wharton School. *"Never expect anyone to act in a manner that serves your values unless you give them adequate reason to do so."* This is a break-through quote. It highlights the need for persuasiveness as the ongoing case, below, describes.

The partners knew the woman in question had two pre-school tots at home, which carried its burden of guilt for her. She also had a full schedule of work as the operating consultant at client sites, a role she preferred. Thus, her priorities or values were two-fold: making sure the kids were cared for; and staying fresh by doing consulting work. To her, partnership possibly meant (1) more time away from home and (2) less actual consulting time with clients and probably administrative work to replace it; thus none of these changes was important or appealing to her . . . not now, anyway. So, what could the partners do? Give up?

One of the most practical theories of motivation is the *Expectancy Theory* (worth a Google look) which explains how individuals theoretically process requests from bosses (spontaneously and sometimes unconsciously and with lightning speed) in order to make a choice of response. Three questions are processed:

1. Can I do the task asked of me? (Do I have the ability?)
2. What's in it for me (WIFFM) if I am successful?
3. Is the implied reward something I value?

Assuming such questions are processed by the consultant in question, her answers might look like this (the bold print shows her primary thinking):

1. **"Yes,** I can do it. I do some of these things now.
2. WIFFM? On the plus side, there'll be more money and prestige but on the negative side, **I'll probably have less time with the kids** (feel the guilt in this thought) and a loss of client contact and hands-on consulting which I love. **Maybe there'll be more desk work, business meetings and non-consulting work.**
3. So, **no,** it's not something I value right now. **Maybe later,** when the kids are bigger, I'll pursue it."

The partners might typically give up on her as a new partner at this point and move on. But, using the Expectancy Theory, watch the imaginary dialogue in *Figure* 19 as the partner tries to change her mind by anticipating in advance what her answers to the basic three questions need to be.

Figure 19: Dialogue Based on Expectancy Theory

The Consultant Processes	The Partner Perseveres
1. Can I do it? "Yes, I can."	"We know you can handle it. We have total confidence in you. You are highly respected by everyone.
2. WIFFM? "The prestige is nice, so is the money. I know I'd feel proud... but being a Mom is more important; they're too young to get less time from me. I'd feel guilty. I'd stop doing what I love most....consulting. Maybe later.	"We all want you to accept. There will be profit sharing and freedom to build your practice as you see fit. You can still be the primary consultant on key accounts. We can give you an Exec Assistant for the desk work. We won't expect you to spend less time with your kids. Temporarily we can get you set up at home and you can work as you spend non-consulting days there. You can achieve what you want and still accept the promotion. I will help you make the transition.
3. Is this something I value? "I see my concerns will be met. It's a win-win. I trust my boss, so the decision is <u>YES</u>!	"We're thrilled with your decision. We'll honour our promises. Now, how shall we announce it?"

What did the managing partner do or say that persuaded her to change her mind? Apart from persevering, an essential part of persuading/motivating, the partner took her values into account and accommodated them in his counter-proposals. He created the perception in her mind that what the partners wanted her to do, i.e. accept the promotion, was something that she would derive value from if the firm could accommodate her needs. They did; she trusted her boss; it was a win-win outcome.

So, *how do you motivate your individual employees*, the first question in this chapter? You imagine each person going through a similar thought process, the same three questions that applied to the consultant, and prepare your persuasive arguments accordingly. Your chances of success are increased if, like the managing partner, you can be trusted to keep your end of the bargain.

A basic human need is also to avoid dissatisfaction. Getting people to do things they'd rather not do could, from time to time, require you to order it done; but, in those circumstances, what you'll mostly get is compliance. Hopefully, these situations will be infrequent. If relationships get testy in such cases and insubordination occurs, it's time to consult with your HR representatives to make sure any disciplinary action follows due process. Most negative behavior is based in the employee's perception that her or his expectations are not being satisfied. Not surprisingly, *boredom* is often a cause of lackluster effort. Other reasons can include the perceived quality of leadership. That is why credible managers with high EQ's do not take such employee behaviors personally. These managers are, by nature, successful at managing relationships and have good character.

So, when deviant behavior is noted, one of the best skills to employ is a proven feedback model shown in *Figure 20* below. It's called the *I-Language Model*, with origins in Parent Effectiveness Training, and it really becomes effective at behavior modification when it is mastered. You can use it anywhere, anytime, when feedback is helpful in reinforcing good behavior or extinguishing poor behavior. It consists of five distinct points to make within the overall goal of feedback:

1. Describe the employee's specific behavior, what was done or not done as the case may be.
2. Describe the effects of the employee's behavior in this case on others or the work.

3. Describe your feelings about what the employee has done or not done, beginning with, "I feel . . ." not, "You make me feel . . . ."
4. Describe the behavior you want from this point forward.
5. Suggest the consequences of giving you the behavior you are requesting.

Figure 20: I—Language Feedback Model

	POSITIVE FEEDBACK	NEGATIVE FEEDBACK
1.	"Your attendance is excellent! You haven't missed any time this month. That's great."	"Your attendance is slipping. You were absent 3 days so far this month and late twice."
2.	"Being on time every day keeps work flow moving. It's also a good example to others."	"When you're absent, others have to pick up your work or we lose productivity. Others complain."
3.	"I'm very pleased. It makes me feel good to give you my appreciation."	"I feel bothered by this. I don't like the feeling I have when I have to remind you of your obligation. I'm disappointed with your tardiness."
4.	"What can I say except keep up the good work"	"What are you going to do about it?" (If non-responsive) "I want you to be here everyday on time. Is that clear?"
5.	"You're a good team member. Thanks"	"Good" I want to be able to give you a good appraisal when the time comes and fixing your attendance problem will help do that"

I include the I-Language Model in my management workshops because it works! I enjoy watching participants develop very persuasive skills once they practice the model using mini-cases I provide. Sadly, I find that few managers know this model and fewer give regular feedback because (a) they're not into giving random feedback, especially praising employees who are supposed to do a good job without being constantly thanked, or (b) they want to avoid the conflict they assume will occur if they offer negative feedback. All I can say is they are missing an opportunity to build a sound relationship and to increase their influencing skills. Credible bosses are good at managing relationships and giving effective feedback. Using the I-Language Model's five key steps will increase a manager's motivational capabilities. Like any skill, delivering feedback in this format takes practice. I use role-playing in my workshops. It takes time to learn how to follow the sequence and to stick only to actual behaviors the person did or didn't act out. The real challenge, as always, is how to handle an employee who takes a defensive position and protects her/himself, a natural expectation grounded in ego. Imagine this dialogue between a manager and an employee:

> Manager: "YourAttendanceisslipping.You'vebeen absent three days and late twice this month!"
>
> Employee: "I was sick! What do you expect me to do . . . come in and spread my germs around? You're being unfair. I've got a good record here. Why are you singling me out?"

Stop! As you can see, the employee is resisting the criticism by defending ego. It's a good ploy if it works and boss backs off. It's called manipulation and managers who don't know how to handle conflict, or avoid it by nature, lose control at this point of the interview. What do credible managers do in situations like this one? They follow established rules of *assertiveness*, hone their confrontational skills and stand up for their rights without violating the rights of the employee.

Among a manager's rights are the right to assign, praise, correct, confront, agree, disagree, to say 'No' without feeling guilty and to be treated respectfully. Likewise, an employee has the right to assert a point of view, ask for help, to disagree, to agree, to defend unreasonable accusations or demands and also to be treated respectfully. Credible managers have acquired relationship-saving skills even when confronting manipulative employees.

Staying on this topic for a moment longer, I often hear the term 'communication problem' used when it really is a situation involving conflict. The term is meaningless. It could mean anything from, 'I don't like you' to 'You're lazy,' to, 'God . . . I'm jealous of you but can't show it,' to 'How I'd like to get rid of you.' But, none of these phrases can be used without increasing the conflict, so people need to rely on better forms of communication. Here's my preferred definition of communication that I believe will serve all managers well:

Communication is the exchange of meaning between two
or more individuals with conflict reduced or removed.

Being skilled, when communicating with others, is the mark of a credible manager. To become this skilful requires a mastery of verbal problem-solving skills available in assertiveness workshops and honed with lots of practice. There's a really old but helpful book titled *When I Say 'No' I Feel Guilty* by Manuel P. Smith that illustrates the kinds of verbal problem-solving skills an assertive manager needs. They really work!

Question 2 at the beginning of the chapter was: *How much time should I spend with my people?* Every time you meet one-on-one with your people, you have a chance to maintain or improve your current relationship. So, apart from an infrequent, 'How're you doing?' or 'How's the family?' the answer about frequency of contact is . . . it depends. One of the more practical theories that I utilize in my workshops is *Situational Leadership* (SLT) made hugely popular by Ken Blanchard, of *One Minute Manager* fame. *SLT*, as it is called, has gone through several iterations since it was posited years earlier by Robert House when he was at the University of Toronto. SLT should be part of every manager's skill set. I have presented it at countless workshops using Blanchard's excellent learning aids. It is always well-received by participants for its simplicity and applicability. For managers, it teaches them three key points:

1. It helps prevent *over-supervising* which comes across as overbearing and distrusting and has a detrimental effect on relationships.
2. Conversely, it prevents *under-supervising* which frustrates those who need but aren't getting enough direction and emotional support.
3. It helps answer the question: 'Who needs more of my time and who needs less?'

I recommend Blanchard's materials on SLT. It's an excellent conceptual framework and has very practical use for tailoring your time and attention to your people according to their needs as related to their tasks. Add the I-Language Model when talking with employees for a one-two punch combination.

Question 3 at the beginning of the chapter was: *'How do I deal with difficult people and low performers?'* Here's another favorite definition I tell managers to store in their memory:

> *Assertiveness means standing up for your rights without violating the rights of others.*

So, what are your rights? It's a long list: the right to be treated with respect, to express your views, expect direct reports to honor their obligations for quality and timely work, for people to follow your legitimate instructions, to decide the work your people perform, to expect employee cooperation, to choose to whom to delegate work; to hire, promote and develop . . . the list is endless in a work situation. And what happens when someone differs with you? There is a chance that conflict will arise.

Let's start with a brief look at conflict in the workplace. It is inescapable and common and managers must expect it and learn how to deal with it. The most useful definition I've heard is from the work of Thomas-Kilmann and goes something like this:

> *We begin to experience conflict whenever something that's important to us—our image, our values, our well being—is threatened.*

Wouldn't it be nice not to have to be concerned about these subjects? But, how realistic is that considering the differences that exist between what we consider important and what others feel? Differences exist over a range of job-related matters: how to do the job, who should do it, how work is assigned and when it must be completed. Add envy, jealousy, unhealthy competition and personal biases and you have a basis for conflict. Read the definition again. Can you recall past conflict involving others at work based on the possible causes shown?

Thomas-Kilmann workbooks and videos on conflict are partly captured in the diagram shown in *Figure 21*. They show the choices a manager has when confronted with conflict. I have borrowed their ideas to make the point.

Figure 21: Conflict Choices

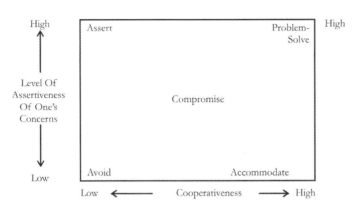

Thus, when you experience conflict, you have five choices in the model in *Figure 21* from which to choose an appropriate response:

1. **Bottom left corner:** In situations where you use *little assertiveness or cooperation*, you are *avoiding* the situation. This is acceptable if the issue is a small one. But, if you are avoidance-prone and don't like unpleasantness, this will not bode well if you are responsible for the performance of others and their behavior leaves you feeling conflicted. This is a very common weakness in managers . . . especially those who like to please and/or dislike confrontation.

2. **Top left corner:** When you are *highly-assertive but not very cooperative* it's all right if you are truly *asserting* your legitimate authority to get something done and the situation calls for it. Otherwise it may be seen as my way or the highway, an example of taking an ego trip e.g. 'because I said so . . . . !'

3. **Bottom right corner:** When you exhibit *low assertiveness and high cooperativeness,* you are *accommodating.* There are many situations where you are easily able to accommodate the concerns of others, and agree with them, because they are right in the circumstances and the outcome is acceptable. This improves relationships. Conversely, managers who cave-in to employees' unreasonable demands or requests, are seen as weak and lose credibility . . . and experience personal conflict.

4. **Centre of the grid**: The mixture of *moderate assertiveness and cooperativeness,* commonly called a *compromise,* is quite acceptable when, in order for both parties to get what they want, they must each give up something. It's not the ideal solution for each but it works. In other words, a workable compromise is mutually reached.

5. **Top right corner:** This is true problem-solving at its best. It takes experience and skill to reach this level of conflict resolution. Both parties get what they want through *the exchange of meaning with the conflict reduced or removed.* This involves the highest level of verbal problem-solving skill, empathy and assertiveness, acquired through lots of practice involving role-plays. Sorry, but you can't get this skilful without practice.

Google the work of Thomas-Kilmann and, if you can find their video, *Dealing with Conflict,* take full advantage of its concepts. Dealing with conflict is part of a credible manager's skills set. Their workshops are also very helpful.

Another HR concept I want to mention is the phenomenon known as the *self-fulfilling prophesy.* It's a concept, not a skill per se, and some would call it a phenomenon. But it explains a great deal as to why people either live-up to or live-down below their potential based solely on our expectation of them! We predict outcomes before they happen . . . and then, they happen as we expected! We judge others based on what we expect, or don't, from them. We think and act in ways that somehow make our expectations of people or situations come true. In human relations in the work place, this can be disastrous. Some managers do not realize how prophesies can become self-fulfilling, even if their prophesies are wrong!

I once watched a video where the facilitator asked the audience:

1. "How many of you managers have people working for you who are A's? You know . . . the ones who are willing and able; the ones with initiative and drive; the ones you can count on?" Hands shot up, faces smiling.

2. "How many of you have B employees? You know them; they show up every day and do their jobs; they're not A's but they're steady and reliable." A majority of hands shot up.
3. "Now, how many of you have C employees . . . . the ones who have little desire or initiative; you'd get rid of them if you could?" Hands shot up with a variety of grimacing faces.

Then, catching the audience off guard, the facilitator asked, "What are you doing to make the C's at least B's and the B's potential A's?" And that little exercise led to the important finding that a manager's expectations of an employee, right or wrong, are somehow communicated through actions, inactions and unconscious body-language to the employee resulting in employee behavior that the manager somehow expected! Then the facilitator described the quality of the interaction felt by the A's, B's, and C's as expressed by *them* in his study:

- A's reported more frequent, friendly, inquisitive interactions with their bosses. They were treated more respectfully; relationships bordered on friendship; the A's were entrusted with more upstream information and given more say in how things were done.
- B's reported less frequent contact with their bosses, mostly on superficial matters related to the job. They were pretty much left alone.
- C's reported the least amount of respect and felt criticized and ignored. Their contact with their bosses was minimal, impersonal and, in some cases, tense.

Look at the differences in the behaviors of the bosses reported by the A's, B's, and Cs! This is the self-fulfilling prophecy at its worst! How can a manager look good if he or she blames results on not enough A's and too many B's and C's? This is why higher-ups wonder about the quality of leadership below. Here's the message: if your people don't look good, what does that say about you? And here's the conclusion of the study: Who do you think—of the A's, B's, and C's—felt the most undervalued? The Bs did! Surprise! What a loss of potential!

So, the message is that employees have the potential to give you better performance . . . if they want to! But why should anyone try harder if they perceive that your expectations of them aren't high? *Potential* is the level of performance an employee could achieve under ideal conditions, as perceived by them. Employees excel in some things and not others and this is the gap you need to close. The size of the gap is a way to determine how much of your attention and effort is needed. At the very least, you must maintain the expected standards of performance dictated by your KRA's and theirs as defined in Chapter 3.

The final HR challenge for you involves another phenomenon: *self-assumed heroism*. This is when a manager, trying to be all things to all people, takes on the responsibilities of others through the misguided belief that it's part of the job. No, it isn't! If you let your people delegate up you'll end up with a time management problem and the stress that accompanies it. So, get *Harvard Business Review* article 99609 titled *Management Time: Who's Got the Monkey?'* It's a classic portrayal of why self-assumed-heroism shouldn't be part of an aspiring manager's profile. This humorous article really puts delegation practices into perspective.

Personal Exercise for Chapter 10

1. Classify your employees according to the A, B, C definitions just discussed. Do this only this one time and never do it again! Now, look at your expectations of these employees. Are you guilty of harboring such self-fulfilling prophesies?
2. Consult Ken Blanchard's SLT materials and decide where each person's development level for each major task is on the SLT matrix. That should tell you with whom, when and for what you need to interact with each person.
3. Find out what each person values in the work place i.e. interests, career aspirations, likes, dislikes, current satisfaction level, concerns, etc. Come up with tasks and activities that will give them what they value if they earn it. Use Hackman and Oldham's materials to examine ways to design work to make it more intrinsically interesting, even if training is required.

Decide the job improvements and changes that are needed that will move C's to B's and B's to A's. Use the A's and B's to help.

4. Master the I-Language Feedback Model and spell out the changes you want each person to make. Get agreement on these changes. Use the same model to give regular feedback on performance. Be generous with deserved praise.

5. Master the concepts on *Dealing with Conflict* as so aptly described by the Thomas-Kilmann materials. Take a workshop on assertiveness if needed.

6. Park your biases and judgments and concentrate on conveying your expectations that each of your employees will succeed and you will help.

7. Value everyone, as hard as that can be at times. Deliver on promises.

8. If all else fails, learn how to terminate with dignity, for which expert help will be needed.

Human resource management is so important that I recommend taking applied workshops where actual interpersonal skills are practiced. And don't be reluctant to read a classic like Dale Carnegie's *How to Win Friends and Influence People* for a refreshing non-academic reminder about basic human behavior and ways you can increase your ability to influence people to want to do their best.

Chapter 11

Maintaining a Great Work Climate

Key Points for this Chapter:

1. *Climate is the workplace as perceived by the people who work there, not their bosses;*
2. *Establish the criteria that stakeholders can agree represent a great place to work;*
3. *Conduct periodic anonymous surveys of your climate and keep it healthy.*

Inevitably, at social functions I, like other professionals I expect, get asked, "What do you do?" I describe my consulting specialty and sometimes hear, "You should see my organization . . . we could sure use some help." It usually ends there because I don't offer free advice, especially when I can't really determine the facts of the matter. But the point these occasional chats suggest is that some people don't like the conditions under which they work . . . and that includes how they perceive their bosses! Does this affect their attitudes? Do they leave? Do they stay and tolerate these conditions? Do they pay back the organization with less than full performance? Here is my favorite definition of climate:

Climate is the workplace as perceived by the people who work there, not their bosses.

Some call it an atmosphere, others say environment, but they're all talking about the place where they work. How important is the workplace climate? Very! Here's a survey I remember from a Korn Ferry report on climate. The following questions were simple enough but the answers were very revealing.

1. When you go to work, is it with the intention of performing your best? Result: 90+% said "Yes."
2. At your current place of work, do you do your best? Result: about 65% said, "Yes."
3. If there's a difference between your answers to questions 1 and 2, what is the reason?

The gap, which was wide, was summed up in the words, 'because the conditions under which we could do our best are very different than the actual conditions we work under now!' And so it goes! Does that highlight the importance of your organization's work climate? Here's another anecdote that provides insight into the importance of climate.

> When I was learning my craft as a trainer in an auto assembly plant, I sold the plant manager on the need for a new supervisory program because of severe turnover. Promotions, at that time, were made from assembly line workers, the assumption being that experience on the line was the most important factor in selecting a new supervisor. This myth is still influences the way that new supervisors are chosen in many industries. Most had little or no formal training as supervisors and our goal was to improve their image and chance of success while helping them through the transition from worker to boss through our learning processes and materials. The course was ten-days long, the curriculum covered all relevant topics and the feedback from participants was off-the-charts. We were ecstatic. There were kudos all round, photos in the company paper, a post-grad party and lots of good will.

Then, within a few months, reality struck. Back on the line, classroom practices fell away. The union pressured the new supervisors; employees tested them and our high expectations crashed, heavily. One of the old hands gave us unsolicited feedback, cynically, as I recall: "What did you expect? For two weeks up there in your fancy quiet classroom they were like fish swimming in an environmentally-pure stream. Then, you packed them up and threw them back into a polluted environment that is toxic. Did you prepare them for that?" It was frustrating and our pride quickly plummeted. We had only worked on our people not our climate!

Google 'Great Places to Work' and you will get a lot of hits and ideas about workplaces that get rave reviews from their stakeholders. The criteria for a great climate are plentiful. One of my previous clients in Ontario made it to the 'Top 50' companies in Canada for five straight years! Her company eventually made it to the 'Top 3' in the whole country! In the survey, employees rated their own company. Did the recognition help attract new people? Did that mean they were successful at developing and keeping good people? You bet it did!

So, the message is clear. You define what a great place, or climate, looks like and make your organization look like the model. You can start small and grow big. You can start with your own section, unit or group. Suppose you created an anonymous questionnaire that announced the intention to make the department as great a place to work as possible. Here's what the questionnaire could ask:

Figure 22: Simple Climate Survey (Anonymous)

1. What do you *like most* about our workplace? Below, list as many features as you can, with at least five items.
2. What *don't you like* about our workplace that we need to look at? Again, list as many features as you can.
3. On the scale below, please circle your overall evaluation of our workplace at this particular time:

Scale: **Awful**   1   2   3   4   5   6   7   **Great**

4. List the most important changes and improvements you believe we need to make to become better and make our scores go as high as possible. Please offer specific examples.

Imagine that you get a decent response and you have a list of everyone's input. Some of the replies will be too vague or general. Some will be negative. Don't concern yourself with that. You can publish this list in no particular order, avoiding duplication for the same or similar ideas, and ask the group members to grade each item as each sees it, using the following triage formula:

3=must improve item
2=should improve item
1=could improve item
0=unimportant to me or OK as is

When the anonymous feedback is received by you, tally the scores using a weighted-average for each item showing all rated factors in order of importance. Publish it. Then you can plan how to start making the changes according to the workplace factors that are within your authority. A search of the internet will likely net you some alternative sample questionnaires that you can use instead of creating the one described in this chapter. It might look like the one below in *Figure 23*.

Figure 23: Department Climate Survey

CLIMATE CRITERIA FOR OUR DEPARTMENT	Score
For each factor, give it a rating using the legend below	
We have or are:	
1. A good <u>reputation</u> with our stakeholders	
2. Clear <u>goals</u> and <u>strategies</u> to achieve them	
3. Clear job <u>responsibilities</u> and <u>authority</u>	
4. Efficient <u>business processes</u> (user friendly too)	
.5. Challenging and fair work <u>assignments</u>	
6. Mutually <u>respectful</u> to each other	
7. Strong <u>team spirit</u> and <u>values</u>	
8. A good flow of timely <u>information</u>	
9. Good working <u>relationships</u> vertically/horzontally	
10. Provided with appropriate <u>learning opportunities</u>	
11. A good sense of <u>accomplishment</u> and <u>pride</u>	
12. Rewarded on the basis of <u>merit</u>	
13. A business climate that is <u>also fun</u>	
14. Able to <u>celebrate</u> successes	
15. Given timely and <u>helpful feedback</u> on performance	
16. Given accommodation for <u>personal difficulties</u>	
17. Excellent <u>salaries and benefits</u>	
18. Part of a <u>respected</u> and <u>successful</u> company	
Scoring Legend 3 = Must Improve 2. = Should Improve 1 = Could Improve 0 = Not a problem	

Designing and applying climate surveys is a service I am paid to do but there's no reason why a manager can't do this if she or he is trusted and has the time to do it. Anonymity has to be guaranteed, of course, or it won't work and, while the respondents remain anonymous, the reported information and scoring is shared openly, and verbatim, to give everyone a view of people's perceptions at any given time. Once published, you ask the respondents for ideas for improvement from their triage scores, i.e. 'For items with a score of 2 or above, list as many changes and improvements as you can that will lower these scores to 1 or 0."

At the end of this exercise you probably will get a host of suggestions, some good and some not, from which you can pare down the list to realistic and achievable improvement targets. Then, within your authority to act, you announce the changes that will be implemented. If there are climate factors you cannot change, for example salaries and perks, explain why and move on. About four months later, send the same blank form out again. Calculate the new scores and circulate the results. Look for a positive trend because some of the climate factors can't be improved or achieved significantly without more time and attention. And don't get suckered by the catch-all term 'poor morale.' It's vague and can't possibly apply to all people. Deal with facts, not opinions . . . and resolve issues one-on-one.

Personal Exercise for Chapter 11

Create and distribute a climate questionnaire using my example or a more sophisticated on-line version. Assure anonymity. Follow the guidelines and publish the results. Fix climate issues within your control focusing on the obvious and easy ones first and broker your boss's approval for items you can't authorize. Remember: this is all about climate and has a major influence on the well-being and support of your people.

Caution: If *you* are the object of complaints in the anonymous survey, like the nasty CFO in Chapter 5, you may need to consult a coach to help increase your self-awareness. Avoid the tendency to think, 'I know who said that.' You could be right . . . or wrong! Watch for the people who like to spread gossip and rumors about people and events. They use hearsay, unconfirmed facts and unreliable comments for reasons of self-interest and ego. Come down hard on violators, especially those who talk about other people's character and private lives.

Imagine what it would be like if you conducted a survey like this twice a year while acting in good faith to correct problems and improve climate. You'd be credible. And don't be afraid of asking these questions because you believe the answers will mostly be negative. If the climate really is that bad, you'll be doing everyone a favor if you start this process immediately instead of sweeping it under the rug. If you are courageous enough to announce a climate survey, you will benefit from using values statements as described in the next chapter.

Chapter 12

Living Core Values

Key Points for this Chapter:

1. *Values represent what the organization believes are the important standards for business behavior;*
2. *Managers must operate from an agreed set of strong, positive operating principles/values;*
3. *Monitoring the adherence to stated values keeps performance on true course.*

Every organization has values whether they are written or not! In *Figure 23,* in the last chapter, values are what the organization members *perceive* are important to live (or not) and are guidelines for behavior. For reasons I cannot fathom, some organizations downplay writing a Values Statement, calling them too soft or fuzzy or touchy-feely. But, observable organization behavior *is* a reflection of its values. So why not live by positive values that help the organization achieve success?

Values are preferred ways of doing things and act as excellent guidelines for day-to-day organizational behavior. They define expected business conduct. They convey an image. As part of my OC work, I have conducted values audits. As the name implies, I try to get a picture to give the executive team of current perceptions about whether the formally-stated values, if there are any, are being lived by the stakeholders. A hypothetical audit is shown in *Figure 24.* The left-hand column shows the values as typically found in organization literature. The right-hand column shows the remarks obtained through this anonymous questionnaire. One glance at the opposing behaviors tells the reader what the gaps are and suggests the changes needed to satisfy the value statement. In other words, the current statement of values is rhetoric and everybody knows it!

Figure 24: Values Audit Survey

STATED VALUES	SURVEY FINDINGS
1. Customers are the reason we exist. We promise on-time delivery and excellent customer service.	We have lost key accounts and market share. We are not innovating. Complaints are higher than normal.
2. Our products bear our name. We commit to the highest quality products with guaranteed performance.	Warranty costs are up and we are getting 15% returns. Delivery is hit or miss.
3. Operating Efficiency is how we control costs to increase our margins.	Cost overruns are common. Machine downtime is up. Overtime is excessive.
4. Our Employees are our most important resource. We will demonstrate respect and offer competitive salaries and benefits and personal development opportunities.	Pay is average. Benefits haven't changed with the times. Promotions scarce. It's not a bad place to work (climate) but some obvious improvements are needed (examples cited).
5. Our Suppliers are important partners; thus we will sustain a value-for-value business relationships.	J.I.T. inventory isn't working. A few key suppliers are over-promising and under-delivering. This affects our delivery capability.

As this hypothetical audit shows, there is a serious gap between what the organization claims it stands for and what behavior it accepts. In this case the organization's stakeholders may ask, "What value is there in having values?" and they act accordingly and, as my more vocal client employees say, "What a load of B.S."

I advocate the writing of value statements. Sure, they describe an ideal condition but what's wrong with having them and measuring adherence to them? Imagine the pride and productivity in a work unit that got full marks for the five values shown in *Figure 24*! This is another example of credible managers working *on,* and not just *in,* their organizations. You have to stand for something. Values help.

I have experienced reluctance by senior managers to create a Values Statement or allow an audit of the ones they have in print. Why such resistance? Here are some of their reasons:

1. 'Let's wait until all of our organizational problems are resolved first; otherwise we'll be roasted in the feedback.'

2. 'If we came out with a new statement of positive values compared to what's accepted now, we'd be laughed at.'

My reactions have been open and blunt: "First off, you have organizational problems *because* of a lack of clear, positive and enforced values. Second, you will continue to be criticized until you change the way things are done around here . . . and changes rely on defining what's important in carrying out your business, i.e. your values."

Suppose you see the merit of operating according to clear and positive organizational values, sometimes called *organizational principles*. You want to get buy-in from your group so they feel a sense of ownership. You ask a small group of opinion-leaders to engage with you in writing draft values. In a facilitated group session, led by you or a qualified facilitator, you can ask the group to ponder and answer three questions:

1. Describe what we have to look like to be seen as a highly-credible organization?
2. At what activities must we particularly excel to be seen by ourselves and others as highly-credible?
3. How can we do this and still have fun?

Assume, for illustration, the final draft of several looks like the details in *Figure 25*.

Figure 25: Our Core Values

We Need To Be	We Need To Excel At:
Effective	We deliver our product/service on time with zero defects. We keep our customers satisfied.
Efficient	We meet or beat our budget. We increase our output within current resource allocation.
Cohesive	Teamwork thrives. We help each other. Conflicts are dealt with quickly and constructively. Trust is high. We work well with other departments.
Progressive	We learn from experience. We innovate and find ways to do our work better. We embrace change.

Doesn't *Figure 25* tell everyone what your unit's core values are, what's important and what you stand for? And do these value statements enable you to measure progress and results? Imagine having a draft document like the one in *Figure 25* and circulating it to your employees, asking:

1. Do you understand these values or do any points need explaining?
2. Can you comfortably support these values?
3. Are there values we missed and need to add?

Imagine, also, that the draft passes review with the inevitable bit of wordsmithing. You can then issue a final draft for consensus, the best definition of which is one from one of Will Schutz' speeches and still find invaluable:

> *In consensus, we all agree to support the decision even if we, acting alone, might prefer to say it or do it differently.*

Thus, consensus is formed around the *intent* of the statement rather than precise semantics, as some people insist on having. What do you do with the values statement? You use it often, parade it, hype it, put it on your letterhead if it fits or at the top of every meeting agenda . . . and then reinforce it. One of my clients likes to ask: "Is what we are discussing or deciding today consistent with our values statement?" If it is, discussion continues; if not, discussion is set aside for another venue.

How do you reinforce your agreed values? Remember the I-Language Model described in Chapter 10? Imagine this scenario in which a credible manager observes one of her employees talking to a customer. When the call is completed, the manager says, "Cindy, I overheard what you said to the customer. You offered to track the order and call back within half-an-hour. That's excellent customer relations. It makes us look good and it's what our values promise. I feel great about your customer approach; so thanks. Keep up the good work." Stop and set a timer. Read the narrative aloud.

What was it? Fifteen seconds? Was it good for the employee? Will it reinforce the core values?

What about a negative scenario? Imagine this feedback from the same manager. "Cindy, I overheard what you said to the customer. It sounded like an argument when you raised your voice and said, 'It's not my fault the order's late; it's the trucking company we use.' That's not our idea of good customer relations. Customers don't want to hear excuses. Frankly, I'm disappointed because I know you're better than that. So, next time, just tell the customer you're sorry and you'll get on it right away. Understand? Agree? Good." Set the timer again and read the dialogue aloud. It only takes 20-25 seconds to reinforce the value system through effective feedback. Does it get the employee back on track? Is it worth 25 seconds of your time?

Honoring the core values is done through the regular observation of employee behavior and the instant feedback, positive and or negative, you give. You use the values statement as the *neutral referee* and they can see how their behavior does or does not measure up to the stated values because they had previously approved the values and agreed to support them. Circulate the values statement every four months and ask each employee to anonymously rate and mail back their perceptions on how each value is being honored and performed. A simple triage method works fine, i.e. we're: 3=exceeding our promise; 2=meeting our promise; 1=below our promise. Ask for written statements describing things to start, stop or continue doing as part of their feedback. Seek ideas for improvement. Publish the feedback and take time to thank people where it is positive.

Remember Anderson's credo*: What gets measured—and rewarded—gets done better next time.* As for the 15-20 second feedback dialogue, described in this chapter, it is often enough to keep performance on track. So, do it often, do it often, do it often!

One final example of the importance of core values is shown in *Figure 26.* It is from a former client of mine who opted to write a Corporate Values Statement in the manner described in this chapter so that everyone would know what the company stood for and how they should act. It made for an excellent speech by the CEO when orienting newcomers and also as a template for feedback on current company performance. Examine it and you'll see how clearly it outlines the measures that will be used to represent organizational excellence. I favor all my clients agreeing to operate with a clear, supported Values Statement. It takes time to create and reach consensus on the intent of the statement, but it lasts a long time and tells the true story of success. Despite the recent problems Johnson & Johnson had with product recalls, J&J's years of consistent success was grounded by their credo which is definitely worth a read on Google or the company's website.

Figure 26: Pictogram of a Client's Corporate Values

Devoted to it's customers
- Meets or exceeds needs
- Is "preferred" over others
- All customers are highly-valued
- Responsive to all requests for information

Involved in Community
- Involved and respected in our communities
- Gives back to targeted needs

Committed to it's people
- Hires the best who put customers first
- Grows talent and rewards performance
- Values fun

Preferred Company Culture

Strongly-Led
- Provides clear vision, direction and structure
- Creates the conditions for excellence
- Builds leaders at all levels
- Cross-functional links are strong
- Leadership is shared

Focused on Strong Performance
- Challenges the status quo
- Intentions become reality
- Sets challenging and motivating targets

Able to Adapt to Changing Conditions
- Forward-looking, sensitive to conditions
- Quick sound decisions
- Change without disruption

Dedicated to Improvement
- Learns and improves from experience
- Recognizes value-added innovation
- Business processes support smart growth
- Tolerant of error

Personal Exercise for Chapter 12

Using the guidelines in this chapter, create a Values Statement for your working unit using group input. Get consensus, publish it and use it as your report card for reaching your preferred future state. Measure the scores, perhaps quarterly, until the need diminishes because of good grades. You'll be glad you did.

Chapter 13

Learning to Learn to Learn

Key Points for this Chapter:

1. *A learning organization keeps in sync with its greater environment;*
2. *Managers must build-in learning processes as part of their monitoring role;*
3. *Experiential learning is a key tool to keep all employees in a learning mode.*

Before discovering full-time OC consulting as my chosen career, I obtained solid HR experience in three major organizations. I fell into the learning business when the head of training at my well-known automaker employer asked to be moved to a different function. I knew nothing about adult education at the time but I accepted the challenge, reasoning the experience would add to and enhance my HR credentials. Although I approached the new job with enthusiasm and was dazzled by the teaching presence of my mentor, it didn't take long for a serious disjoint to arise between what was taught in class and what the students were still unable to do on the job! Why? Because, our emphasis had been on *delivery*. We took train-the-trainer courses, role-played teaching skills, memorized content, created case studies, produced lots of visual aids and materials and honed our presentations. It was like preparing for a play. We knew what we were going to do. In class, we were the actors. It was an ego trip. If students didn't get it, it was their fault. This inert stance wouldn't have moved if it hadn't been for the visit by a head office consultant and the feedback he gave us after observing us in action. One of his remarks struck home when he said, "You guys seem to think you're in the teaching business, but you're not! *You're in the learning business.* Once you make this important mind shift you'll see a difference." He was right and we did. It took a lot more time and effort but it worked.

In Quinn's model in Chapter 4 one of the key roles of a manager is monitoring. That involves critical-thinking which enhances learning. Remember the theme that runs through this book: work *on* your organization, not just *in* it? That's what our experience in the automotive training function showed us once we thought our way out of the rut we were mistakenly reinforcing. The tool the visiting consultant used was the Learning Loop, or Experiential Learning Cycle as shown in *Figure 27.*

Figure 27: The Experiential Learning Cycle

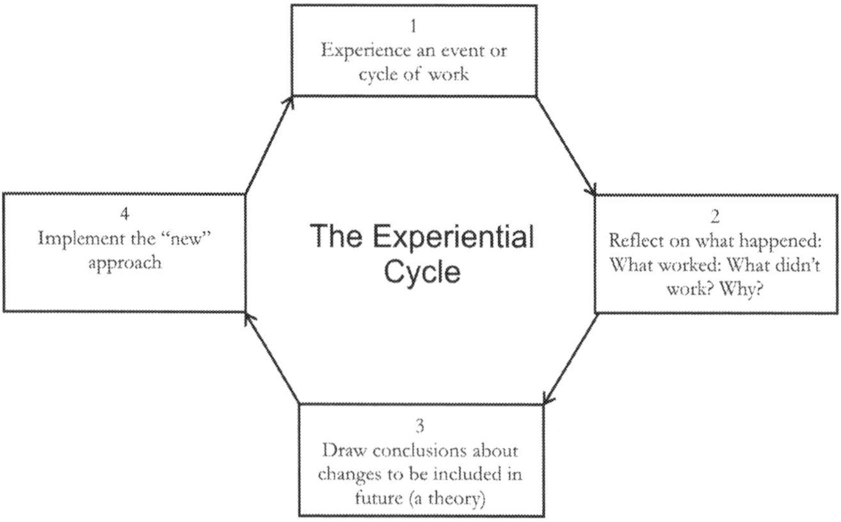

When we were processed through this model with guidance from the consultant we became struck with its simplicity. We learned that we had become talking heads, a persistent fault in education. True, we asked questions to provoke thinking, just as Socrates did; but when the students couldn't or wouldn't speak—a natural phenomenon—we broke the deafening silence by giving away the answer, just as Socrates didn't! We were not enabling the participants to think and hence learn. We did it for them—eloquently, we thought. Thus: *No thinking=no learning!* When the consultant took us through the steps of the model in *Figure 27,* he asked questions and kept us on track but not once did he utter an opinion. What kind of instructor was he, we wondered? And then, when his whiteboard was full of our input, he asked each of us, "What conclusions have you reached and what needs to be done about it?" This happened years ago and I still feel his impact on my learning approach with clients.

I didn't realize the full power of the model until we were asked to facilitate a meeting with company recruiters who were considering participation in a local prominent Job Fair. This had never been tried before because the name of my employer was well-known and respected. Maybe a little corporate ego had prevented participation in a Job Fair in the past but the labor market was tight and too many vacancies remained unfilled. A team of five recruiters was sent to the Job Fair as observers. Based on what they learned after debriefing, using us to facilitate the model, they were able to design a unique approach to a larger Job Fair scheduled in a few more weeks. Processing through the model, here's what they revealed:

1. **Experience an Event:** Over twenty companies took part in the Fair they observed. Some had elaborate booths, showed impressive videos, handed out glossy brochures, distributed job applications, for immediate completion if possible, and hyped their organization's climate and conditions. Some brought new employees to give testimonials. In two days the spin was impressive.
2. **Reflect on What Happened:** Each recruiter was asked by us to reflect on a number of questions about their visit, to prompt critical-thinking. They were each asked:
   a. Who were the best recruiters you saw?
   b. What did they do that made them the best? Give specific examples.
   c. What was the most unique exhibit you saw and why?

    d. Describe some of the novel materials you saw and why you think they were effective.

    e. Who were the worst recruiters and why?

    f. What approaches at the fair didn't work?

    g. What have we forgotten to ask you that you want to add?

3. **Draw Conclusions:** a.k.a. your theory on how we can conduct a successful Job Fair:

    a. What should we do at our fair and why?

    b. What should we not do and why?

    c. What best practices should we be sure to utilize?

    d. How can we top our biggest competitor?

4. **Agree on the Plan:** Brainstorm as a group and choose the 'Top 7' practices to use.

It took the best part of a day to process the five recruiters through each step of the model. At the Job Fair, a month later, the company excelled in every way imaginable. The recruiters attributed their success to the experiential learning model shown in *Figure 27*. When we debriefed the experience, we asked the group: "Was there a key step in the model that made a difference to the outcome?" "Yes," the five responded. "It was step two, reflecting on what happened, that made the difference! Before, when we experienced something, we'd go right to conclusions. But when you take time to reflect on what you observed, you are forced to think critically. Then conclusions become more objective. Opinions are too subjective; they need to be informed. Opinions, generated by reflection, are more credible. Conclusions become more objective.

Credible managers can and should promote experiential learning for the work that goes on in their units. Any business procedure that has a beginning and an end can be processed through the model from time to time. The result: you'll either confirm that what you're doing is effective and efficient, or you'll see areas for improvement. So, scrap jumping to conclusions or trading opinions and add some rigor to your thinking.

Personal Exercise for Chapter 13

Use the experiential model to facilitate your staff through one of your processes or repetitive work cycles and see what conclusions you reach about improvement. Remember: spend some time on reflection/critical thinking at step 2 before going through the rest of the cycle and make sure you get consensus. Then, apply the same discipline to all of your processes based on their current performance results.

Chapter 14

Advocating Well-Managed Change

Key Points for this Chapter:

1. *Change is inevitable and managers need to be good at introducing and managing change;*
2. *Perfection may be unrealistic but best possible performance isn't!*
3. *Improvements in organization performance are always noticed at the top.*

Managers are expected to be brokers of change. In Chapter 4, Quinn's model makes this point. Introducing and managing change successfully, i.e. effectively and efficiently, is a critical management skill and expectation. Credible managers don't simply react to problems and wait for the next one; they eliminate/manage causes. True, the challenge of continuous improvement is operationally difficult, but it's theoretically possible. Thus, the expectation that a manager can manage change is an organizational reality. Managers rationalize when they say, "If it ain't broke, don't fix it." My bias says, "If it ain't broke, can it be done more efficiently, i.e. in less time with fewer resources, employee buy-in, better quality, or not done at all?" That often slows their argument.

Organizational renewal became a fad term in management jargon. It was met with mixed reviews but those who understood the importance of organization effectiveness accepted the need for renewal. However, their rationalization was more of a homily: 'We can always improve.' Look at these Webster definitions:

1. "Renew is to make or become new, fresh or strong again; to restore to existence; to begin again.
2. Renewal means capable of being renewed by sound management practices."

Remember the KRA's from Chapter 3? Imagine that your boss added a new KRA that asked for measurable incremental improvements in *all* of your current KRA's? Wow! Wouldn't you have to spend time *on* your organization? Even if you used the ratchet principle, cranking up change a notch at a time, there are obvious places to start managing change, sometimes called the 'orders of change.'

Order One: *Low Level Change*: Work on obvious deficiencies in performance: *Do the things you're doing now but make sure you are doing them right!* These refer to current activities that are being performed inefficiently. This is where many managers spend most of their time. The term 'firefighting' comes to mind and some managers feel they have accomplished change as and when the fires are put out. But unless the causes of the fires are removed or reduced, there's hardly a defense to the challenge, "Why isn't this working?" So, fixing things that aren't working right is an obvious place to start managing change but it's only the beginning.

Order Two: *Stabilizing Change.* When the deficiencies in performance are resolved at Order One and performance returns to normal, the second stage of introducing and managing change is to decide if *normal* is acceptable. The goal in this step is to perform only the activities that are *essential* which requires removing the non-value-added steps in any process. People become married to routines so taking activities out of the work process is part of Order Two. This step focuses on *doing the right things right.*

Order Three: *Innovative Change:* Once activities are stable at Order Two and all KRA's are being satisfied, the challenge of organizational renewal means looking for better ways to do work with a view to becoming newer, fresher and stronger. This is *innovation*. This is where managers can greatly enhance their potential for advancement. You get a lot of credit if you are a change agent of this magnitude.

How can a manager promote renewal? Here's one example: whenever I conducted an organization review, I asked for permission to facilitate meetings with employees who were performing the work. A group of ten employees spent up to three hours with me to mine the ideas of the group for renewal. It worked every time because most employees already know the obvious changes that should be made in their workplace. Too often, employees resign themselves to the way things are because their bosses don't give these roadblocks, except the urgent ones, much attention. I asked the group members after promising their anonymity, "What changes and improvements, if feasible, would make your unit work better?"

I gave them time to work alone, asking each person to identify a minimum of six (6) opinions. Then, I took one idea at a time from each person in round-robin style and wrote it on a whiteboard. When all the ideas (often numbering in the twenties and thirties) were listed the group was led through the following steps:

1. The list was scanned and unclear ideas explained by the employee-author. Duplicate items were removed. No discussion was sought at this step.
2. Individually, they assigned a personal rating to each item on the whiteboard as follows: *3=must do, 2=should do (after 3's), 1=could do (after 2's) and 0=needn't do* (not a problem).
3. The total scores for each item were added and divided by the number of group members resulting in a rank-order averaged weighting from most important to least important to-do items.
4. For each item, the group suggested ideas on how the change should be made and by whom.

This exercise always produces ideas for change. The triage ranking shows the relative importance of the items. Periodic meetings with the group are used to examine the initial list and to keep the agreed changes in motion. This is powerful stuff. Employees have the answers and it's a form of recognition that costs nothing but returns plenty. On persistent issues, you can also process the job holders through the Experiential Learning Cycle described in Chapter 13. Both processes keep the subject of change on the table.

What about the manager's role in innovation? I recommend using Quinn's model from Chapter 4 as a guide to this important role. For each of Quinn's eight management roles I have shown sample changes that a hypothetical manager might choose at a given time. *Figure 28* lists the changes that have been selected for each of the management roles. Every ninety days, when I was in the auto manufacturing business, we had to update our list and give it to the boss for review. Talk about effective . . . and motivating! Try this exercise as a means of paying attention to all eight of your management roles. It works.

Figure 28: 90-Day Improvement Activities

ROLES	CHANGES/IMPROVEMENTS
1. Producer	Adopt Priority Manager software for managing emails & events. Work "on" the organization.
2. Director	Implement 90-day goal-setting and review for each employee.
3. Coordinator	Establish an ad hoc team to examine and recommend more efficient horizontal handoffs; create a RACI chart for all staff.
4. Monitor	Measure own KRA achievement monthly. Utilize the Experiential Learning Model after major process cycles.
5. Facilitator	Introduce employee brainstorming meetings using the Experiential Learning Model. Model a process for dealing with team conflict.
6. Mentor	Create an Individual Development Plan (IDP) for each employee based on SLT. Use "I" language feedback model to manage employee behaviour (as opportunity arises).
7. Innovator	Form a Quality Team responsible for quarterly review of activities and mandate to identify improvements.
8. Broker	Bargain for essential resources; use personal power ethically; increase presentation skills; get appointed to senior management task force team on organization improvement.

As this chapter states, a credible manager is expected to innovate and broker change to achieve improvements to the status quo. Utilizing employees as shown in the above processes is essential. The mantra for a credible manager is a simple one: *Change is possible; change is necessary; well-managed change will succeed.*

Personal Exercise Chapter 14

1. Make your own list of changes that you feel are needed in the workplace. Hold on to it.
2. Facilitate a group of employees (7-10) and process them through the 4-steps described in this chapter. Use a guest facilitator if this is not your forte or there is concern about employee openness.
3. Alone, compare your list to their list and choose the top 5 items for the initial group to work on. After giving the group a look at their input, engage them in discussing each of the top 5 items by asking the question, "In how many ways can we achieve this agreed change?"
4. The results are published and the responsibilities and time lines for change are assigned.
5. Monitor progress and report to the group periodically.

PART THREE

Bonus Strategies that Accelerate Success

Chapters:

Chapter 15

Finding a Good Mentor

Key Points for this Chapter:

1. *You don't find good mentors; they find you . . . if you are worthy;*
2. *An inquisitive mindset and continued high performance attracts genuine mentors;*
3. *There are lots of role models that can help you fashion your management approach and increase your attractiveness for promotion.*

Mentoring goes far back in history and has had staggering success in furthering knowledge and enabling innovation in countless fields of endeavor. The foundations of Philosophy began with Socrates who mentored Plato who mentored Aristotle and passed on the findings to successive generations. If you know the Impressionist Period of Art (1800-1880) you'll realize that mentoring was the process for creating the collections of art that are featured in galleries world-wide. Of the noted Impressionists, Pissaro was mentored by Gleyre; Pissaro then mentored Monet, Sisley and Renoir and these three mentored Gaugin and Cezanne. The point is that the acquisition of excellence is accelerated . . . if you are lucky enough to find a good mentor.

Finding a good mentor is a goal in itself. If you manage to get one or two significant mentors in your career it will make a huge difference in the speed and quality of your development. That's the good news. But, there is a caveat: *Good mentors are scarce and, if there are people you know like this, you will not choose them . . . they will choose you!* Sure, there are potential teachers out there but a good mentor is scarce because to be one requires empathy, sensitivity and a personal value that gives meaning in helping others succeed. These qualities disqualify a lot of people above you even though they mean well. There are a lot of smart managers out there but most are focused on their own upward mobility and job success. Giving time and talent to aspiring managers is not a choice they would make if *not* mentoring was an option.

The worst experience I endured was as a new consultant with a then 'Big-Eight' management consulting firm. Each of the partners was assigned new consultants as a matter of policy. This was done with good intentions but without considering who wanted to be a mentor and was good at it. It was a game of charades and many of the matches failed. Truth was, some of the partners needed mentoring themselves for obvious skill gaps. My assigned mentor was one of these poor choices. The experience was a waste of time for both of us but the policy was clear and the drudgery continued. Until, that is, I was loaned from the HR practice to a senior partner in a different consulting specialty who needed an HR person for a short term assignment out of the country.

This partner was a legend in his industry; successful, well-known and highly-respected across Canada, the USA and internationally. He was a recognized authority on management in this industry and a master at business development i.e. selling consulting services. As a newcomer, I was neither of these and I felt intimidated in his presence early on in our relationship. I knew I was being tested when he dispatched me to my first-ever solo assignment out-of-country. His parting words as I left for the airport were, "If you're any good, you'll survive." Fortunately, I had several years of HR depth from three distinct industries but what I didn't know about consulting, especially client management, was pretty large.

My mentor's dominant leadership style was *delegation* which, in the light of my newness to the profession, seemed paradoxical. Hersey and Blanchard's Situational Leadership Theory *(SLT)*, popular at the time, maintained that a leader should match his or her style to the employee's development level, a combination of competence and commitment to do the task. Theoretically, SLT made sense but my new boss's caution, "If you're any good, you'll survive," presumed that when faced with a succeed or fail option, a qualified person with transferable skills and high self-esteem would rise to the occasion, exceeding his or her own expectations. Talk about creative energy! I felt stretched, became creative, worked extra hours, stayed late, arrived early, felt the tension and the fear of failure. The learning curve was steep, his criticisms blunt. I experienced an approach-avoidance mentality in the very early stages. I made mistakes by assuming what the client needed and how I should plan my work. He cured me of this habit with the perpetual question, "Do you know that for a fact?" In hindsight, it is a great question. When I said, "I think so," he stung me with his criticism. Yet, every interaction with him left me wiser and more confident. Over time, he mellowed. Was I getting smarter? Passing his test? Over the next few years our relationship grew from him being my boss to mentor, to dear friend and business partner.

It came to me later that his test of me was really a test for him! He was deciding whether to devote interest, time and advice in a way that would accelerate my development. I realized that he had decided to be my mentor because he felt I had earned it. SLT theory aside, did it work? We worked together on several major international assignments over the next five years and the experience with his guidance made all the difference to my career and achievement. Eventually, I resigned and opened my own firm. That was the outcome of his enormous impact on me. He introduced me to the profession of management consulting and I loved it. I respected him as a mentor, colleague and friend. When he retired at the mandatory age of sixty-five, he asked to work with me on my assignments . . . as a colleague, not as my boss. On occasion, when students in my business class asked me, "Where do you get all this knowledge of organizations?" I often mentioned my mentor and told them that he was my inspiration for learning my profession and loving every minute of it. I never forgot to thank him, often, right up to the time he passed away. The family asked me to deliver the eulogy.

So, if you can attract a mentor to want to devote time to your development, this person will have to see something about her or himself in you to make it happen. I know, because, despite several requests from others for me to be their mentor, I have only met two people I felt I wanted to help—and did—and we remain good friends. I am truly proud of their accomplishments. This idea of attraction to one's mirror image may seem egotistical but mentoring time is a scarce commodity not to be wasted. *Earn your mentor.*

Personal Exercise for Chapter 15

You already have quasi-mentors about you. Just watching the successful managers around you is educational. But you will attract willing mentors by demonstrating your potential to move up in the organization. Keep habitual self-development as a priority. Express your eagerness to learn and grow. Go after stretching experiences. Volunteer for task forces and ad hoc committees. Get to know potential mentors. Ask them for advice. Sense the relationship: is it growing? Is their interest in your work evident? Do they seem to respond willingly? Remember: you don't choose mentors; they choose you. But, get one if you can.

Chapter 16

Managing Your Boss

Key Points for this Chapter:

1. *You need to accept the importance of being good at managing up as well as down;*
2. *A workable relationship with your boss is an essential measure of your perceived maturity;*
3. *Your boss's delegation power can enhance your growth and preparation for top management.*

Managing *down* into the organization below is hard enough for all managers, but you also have to be effective at managing *up*. Done the right way, this isn't playing politics (although there will always be some of that going on) and it is expected of you by your boss and the bosses of your boss. When I talk about this topic, some people ask me, "Isn't this just sucking up?" Or, I've heard, "If I can't be recognized on my merit, I'm not going to play games to move ahead." That's not what this chapter is about. It's about the critical relationship between you and your boss that already exists! It is critical for both of you, so how can you make it work?

How does your performance affect your boss? Here are some things to remember: She or he:

- Has more responsibility and authority than you
- Has a network of managers above you whose support you may need when you're ready to move up

- Can help or hinder your career
- Can choose to mentor you to accelerate your mobility—or not!
- May already be touting your potential to other managers—or not!
- Is busy doing things you don't even know about and won't
- May be pushing your buttons to see how well you can handle more responsibility
- May have a difficult boss
- May be upwardly mobile and eager to be spoken well of
- May expect you to show your stuff without the expectation of frequent strokes (a common expectation)
- May have doubts about your potential

So, with all of these possibilities, and more, you need to understand pretty quickly what makes your boss tick and to adopt a *complementary* style. The nature of your relationship should be simple: you act in ways that give you both what you need . . . a value-for-value relationship. That, you've got to figure out!

Before you think, 'but you don't know my boss,' relax. Usually, that kind of thinking reveals a lack of understanding of what the boss's expectations really are. Whether you have a great or a lousy boss, you still need to maintain the best possible relationship. Yes, you will have bad days, which could be a clue to the boss's day and you may feel the sting of unjust criticism; your daily priorities may be interrupted by another of your boss's urgent tasks; it may all seem unreasonable, but you still have to maintain a working relationship. That's not politics, that's just common knowledge. Here are some thoughts on that subject.

Start with this test. If you and your peers were managing your assigned KRA's satisfactorily, what would be left over for your boss to do? Answer this question and you may see where opportunities exist for you to manage *up*. You will if you take the time to imagine what your boss's to-do list might look like.

Your Boss's To-Do List:

1. Getting expected results from all direct reports
2. Managing her/his boss where the stakes are higher
3. Creating forward strategy, a clear purpose and direction for your organization
4. Ensuring an internally healthy and productive organization
5. Living the espoused values of the organization
6. Managing through the process of relationships with all stakeholders
7. Protecting her/his direct reports from unfair words or acts
8. Communicating downstream information up
9. Communicating upstream information down
10. Acquiring a fair share of resources for her/his department
11. Managing a succession plan for eventual vacancies
12. Chairing high-level committees
13. Representing the organization with external parties i.e. customers, governments, industry peers
14. Steering achievement of the results expected in the corporate strategy
15. Managing an unreasonable boss (which is not out of the question)
16. This list can be endless

So, assuming your boss is absorbed by any or all of these challenges, the point of this chapter is: What can you do to be supportive to your boss while getting credit for it at the same time?

Your Complementary Support List

1. Stay credible by meeting or exceeding your assigned responsibilities (KRA's)
2. Make sure that key horizontal relationships with your management peers are coordinated and cooperation is evident, especially with those who report to the same boss as you
3. Contribute ideas for the boss to use at the strategy level
4. Ask your boss for genuine advice

5. Volunteer to sit on committees that link to department effectiveness
6. Chair cross-functional committees that deal with corporate-wide issues while keeping your boss informed about decisions and pending discussions of importance
7. Look for and recommend changes and improvements that will increase efficiency/effectiveness
8. Ensure you and your people are living the core values
9. Maintain outstanding employee relations as a standard for others
10. Support top management's goals and vision but not blindly; never bad-mouth top management
11. Give your boss a heads-up on expected deviations from the norm . . . sooner than too late
12. Always make a persuasive business case for resource requests
13. Have an acknowledged successor in training to replace you
14. Find out what management tasks your boss has mastered that no longer present a challenge and ask to be given some of these for your own development for future moves
15. Offer to do tasks that compensate for your boss's known weaknesses or dislikes. (Offering to sit on and chair committees was, for me, a breakthrough).
16. Do not tolerate intimidation tactics by your bosses. Not now; not ever. Call them on it and enjoy the respect it brings from them and others.

"But, I'm busy," you might say, or you might be thinking, "are you crazy?" My reply would be, "If all of your people are doing their jobs satisfactorily and goals are being met, it's time you changed your routine. Go look at the above suggestions and agree that they are the kinds of activities you need to start if you are serious about moving up."

A Case in Point:

> My mentor from the last chapter started delegating tasks to me that were definitely stretch assignments. I began chairing meetings that he had previously

chaired and the pressure mounted as the committees differed in importance and composition. I can honestly say that had he not trusted me and asked me to take on some of his responsibilities, I probably would not have learned how to facilitate meetings. Now, thanks to being allowed to take-on my boss's activities, much of my consulting work involves facilitating management meetings.

So, getting ready to move *up* in your organization, or *out and up* in someone else's, includes managing your boss as suggested. And, if you can't manage these activities sincerely in a value-for-value respectful manner, then most bosses above you will be able to tell the difference between your feigned sincerity and kissing butt!

Personal Exercise Chapter 16

Start noticing what makes your boss tick. Get a feel for her/his KRA's and the difference in breadth and depth of organizational challenges at that level. Show empathy then see how you can add to your current credibility by choosing to change your routines as outlined in this chapter. Remember to ask your boss for both genuine advice and delegated tasks as preparatory work for upward mobility.

Chapter 17

Mastering Your Mind Thoughts

Key Points for this Chapter:

1. *If the results of your behavior, over time, are not meeting your needs, you may be operating under false beliefs and attitudes (mind-thoughts);*
2. *You need to bring your underlying beliefs and attitudes up to a level of self-awareness and challenge them;*
3. *You need to replace old truths with new truths and feel the difference it makes.*

Working in as many organizations as I have for so many years I have met countless managers, most of them competent and confident. But, I've also met managers who failed and left their organizations. Some were fired because of a lack of *fit*, a metaphor for inability and/or lack of character. Some managers remain uncomfortable in their management roles or are tentative at best. Since a great deal of success, or lack of it, is driven by *mind thoughts* (the attitudes and beliefs managers possess about the likelihood of being a success) I've chosen to share a story about a young woman whose results at work were not satisfying her needs. And, it's mostly all about the way she thinks!

Jane was a newly-appointed manager in the Customer Service unit of a major parts distributor. A college graduate, Jane had no clear career goals upon graduation so she accepted a job as a customer service rep in a parts distributor, just to get employment. She could look around for a better job later, but, with student loans to pay, this job would do. She liked the company and they liked her. So she stayed, learning the ins and outs of the parts business and became a product specialist in the process. Four years flew by and when the department manager's job became vacant, Jane applied and won.

"A natural for the job," her boss told his management peers. "She's personable, competent and committed . . . someone with high ideals." Jane's co-workers liked her and always had and seemed happy with her promotion. No one could fault her work ethic or her performance as a product specialist. Several had gone to Jane whenever they needed help on a work problem. Jane put in long hours and was on top of her game as a service rep. But how would she fare as the new manager? No one doubted she'd succeed.

For the first few months all seemed normal; but by the fifth month cracks began to appear in department efficiency and employee productivity. Jane's employees dropped subtle hints at first that her demands seemed unreasonably high. Her boss began to note the declining performance: customer orders were late, some were only partial shipments, there were inventory gaps and returns were up. Now, employees stopped being subtle and became vocal! Jane was fire-fighting most of the time, they said, and often resorted to tirades about mistakes without specifying who was at fault. She lapsed into a micro-managing style, seemingly obsessed with perfection. It appeared she was spending more and more time getting less and less done. Now, it was her indecision the employees were criticizing, claiming that her knee-jerk reactions were making the situation worse! Jane became withdrawn . . . not the outgoing

Jane everyone remembered. She was clearly having a struggle as evident by her overheard remark, "Maybe I'm just not cut out to be a manager."

Jane's boss offered her a potential solution. "I know a good consultant who offers coaching advice to managers. There's no formal management development program here, so I can sponsor you for personal coaching. This will help you through the transition period, I feel sure." Jane agreed.

When the appointed coach gave Jane feedback on all the issues reported to him, Jane simply nodded assent. Once a comfort level was achieved and the matter of confidentiality assured, Jane revealed her frustrations. "I've never felt so ineffective and alone," she said. "Everything I've tried to do has failed. I've tried to do everything perfectly yet I feel guilty all the time for the mistakes we're making as a unit. I fear things before they happen. I try to please everybody, but they all seem to be mad at me. I've overlooked employee errors to avoid conflict and most of the time I feel anxious. I try to appear in control, but I know that's not true. I'm frustrated and confused . . . I don't know what to do."

"Okay," answered the coach, "let me give you some feedback. First off, you are acknowledging a very important principle: the results of your actions are not meeting your own or your people's needs. Is that fair?" Jane agreed. The coach placed a diagram in front of her *(see Figure 29).*

Figure 29: Do the Results You Get Meet Your Needs?

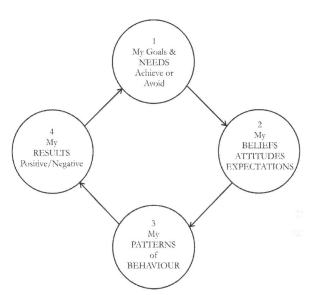

"Let me take you through this behavioral model," continued the coach, "and see how it may apply to your situation." His explanation followed.

"**At step 1**, all people have basic needs: security, affiliation, acceptance, feeling important, achieving success, good health, a good family life, career success, those sorts of things. The list is long. Each person has her or his own needs even though similar needs are shared by many. But they vary in degree and not all are the same or we wouldn't be individuals. In a minute we'll look at your needs, okay?

At step 2, people acquire, through learning from childhood, certain beliefs about how to achieve or meet their needs. They acquire a host of personal attitudes that are related to their perceived needs, now called expectations. These beliefs and attitudes about how to achieve their needs lead to patterns of behavior they learn and rely upon to try to meet their needs.

At step 3, these habitual ways of behaving either get them what they want, or not. Think of this example: If I believe that conflict is bad, I will avoid it at all cost. Make sense? And if I believe that success comes from hard work and I want to be successful, what am I likely to do? What if I believe promotion is political and only favorites get noticed? How might I behave then? What if I learned not to trust people in authority? How might I behave?

At step 4, after behaving in certain ways that to us make sense, either our needs are satisfied or they're not. And if the results of our behavior, over time, consistently fail to meet our basic needs, then is it possible that we are operating with faulty beliefs and attitudes? Remember the definition of foolishness, i.e. doing the same things over and over but not getting the results we want?"

Jane understood the premise of the model in *Figure 29* and the coach moved to the next step: what were Jane's basic needs and were they being met? Here in *Figure 30* is the product of their dialogue.

Figure 30: Jane's Current Needs Gaps

Exercise 1	Jane's Goals/needs	Valid/ Realistic	Being Met?
1.	Acceptance/Belonging	Yes	No
2.	Positive Relationships	Yes	No
3.	Feeling Valued/Important	Yes	No
4.	Variety/Interest	Yes	?
5.	Career Achievement	Yes	No
6.	Health & Happiness	Yes	?
7.	Family	Yes	Yes

Jane agreed that the needs in *Figure 30* were her important needs and her self-disclosure to her coach revealed that many of the most important ones, especially those having to do with her ego needs, were not being met.

"Okay," said the coach; "so whatever you're doing, your day-to-day behavior, can we agree it's not giving you what you want?" Jane agreed. Then the coach moved to **step 2** of the model *(Figure 29)* and said, "Let's dig into your mind thoughts, your belief system, and see if you are acting on any possible false beliefs." *Figure 31* shows the product of their examination of **step 2**: attitudes and beliefs, from a coaching process that might take several meetings.

Figure 31: Jane's Old Beliefs vs. New Beliefs

EXERCISE 2 JANE WAS TAUGHT OR LEARNED	JANE'S NEW BELIEFS
1. Everything I do must be perfect	This is unrealistic! Too many uncontrollable variables can occur.
2. I cannot disappoint others	People have competing values. Differences cannot be avoided.
3. I am no better than others	I am responsible for my behaviour. That's my focus.
4. There are people better than me	"Better" is a vague term. I accept people as I find them.
5. Conflict is a sign of failure	Conflict is inevitable and may be healthy if it leads to win-win solutions.
6. Failing is not an option	Failure will occur. Learn from it and move on.
7. Don't show emotions	It is unnatural and unhealthy to suppress emotions. You don't have to appear "cool" all the time.
8. Accept Responsibility	You are accountable for your own actions, not others.
9. Avoid Criticism	I can use constructive criticism to learn and grow. Welcome it.
10. Don't Disclose Insecurities	Self-disclosure shows honesty. It proves you're human.

At the end of this exercise, Jane was asked the key question, "What does this table *(Figure 31)* tell you about the attitudes and beliefs you have that influence your behavior?"

"That I've been operating under some faulty beliefs for some time and didn't know it," Jane replied.

"Good," said the coach, "because I've got a final exercise for you before I leave you alone for a trial period. I'm only a cell phone call away but for now let's agree on some new behaviors you're going to try based on the changes in your old belief system in *Figure 31.*" Together they produced *Figure 32* shown below.

Figure 32: Jane's Breakthrough New Behaviours

EXERCISE 3 JANE'S NEW BELIEFS	JANE'S BREAKTHROUGH BEHAVIOUR
1. Perfection is unrealistic; obsession with it is anxiety - producing; too many uncontrollable variables are involved.	I will maintain high but attainable standards and do the best possible.
2. People have competing interests and values. Differences will occur.	I will seek to understand these differences and consider them before I act.
3. I am responsible for my behaviour - not others.	I will act responsibly and manage my behaviour.
4. People have different strengths and weaknesses.	I will try to understand and respect these differences in my interactions with others.
5. Conflict is inevitable and may be healthy if it leads to win-win outcomes.	I will approach conflict as a natural by-product of managing and will see workable compromises and win-win results.
6. Failure will occur. Learn from it and move on.	I will install a learning process if failure occurs so that we can eliminate future causes.
7. It is unnatural and unhealthy to suppress emotions. I don't have to be "cool" all the time (especially when I'm not).	I reserve the right to assert my feelings; to express joy, sadness, elation or disappointment. I will not direct demeaning remarks to others, but I will state my concerns.
8. I will accept responsibility.	I accept responsibility for my actions and will do the job to the best of my ability.
9. I can use constructive criticism to learn and grow.	I will invite constructive criticism and act on legitimate information.
10. Indecision can be the best decision in certain circumstances.	I will make calculated risks and avoid hasty, unsupported decisions.
11. Disclosing insecurities is human.	I'll admit it when I don't know what I don't know.
12. When people criticize me it's all about them, not me. It's their problem they're acting out. They don't control my feelings, I do!	I will not take things people say about me personally.

"Where did number twelve come from, Jane?" asked the coach. Jane answered, "I've always felt insecure throughout my life. It's hard to shake and I've always feel the sting when I hear people make negative remarks about me. So, if it's time to get rid of faulty beliefs and attitudes, that's why I wrote number twelve."

"All right," replied the coach, "only two more questions before I leave you to work through the attitudinal and behavioral changes we've agreed on. Ready? One, what have you learned about yourself in the course of our discussions?"

"I've been operating in a pretty narrow rut on a lot of false beliefs, attitudes, assumptions and expectations. I see the connection between my beliefs and my behavior. I have to change the way I think, or my mindset, before I can change my behavior. So, I need to change the way I used to think. It's quite a revelation. I've got a lot to digest."

"Great," replied the coach, "but before I take my leave, here's one more challenge. Do you ever engage in negative self-talk where the voices in your head make you feel sad, guilty, insecure, angry or even hopeless?"

"Sure," Jane answered, "who hasn't?"

"Well, I want you to recognize these negatives when they arise and for each negative thought I want you to think of an empowering positive thought . . . a positive statement about yourself you know to be true. Got it?"

"Yes, I can do that; any other tips?"

"Yes, one more. I want to give you a homework assignment. Forgive yourself for harboring all those negative thoughts and false beliefs and assumptions. Don't blame your parents, your teachers or anybody else. Then make a list of your most positive traits . . . at least a dozen. Add to this list over time. Show it to me in four months when we met again. Remember, if you get rid of your false beliefs and assumptions and change your attitudes that spring from them, you *will* change your behavior. And here's the payoff. If the results of your future behavior, over time, satisfy your basic needs, then you'll know you're operating from the right beliefs and attitudes."

Personal Exercise for Chapter 17

If you can relate to the story of Jane and find that your behavior over time is not consistently meeting your needs, you'll benefit from a coaching session to raise your level of self-awareness of your limiting beliefs. Or, you can try self-coaching by duplicating the exercises in this chapter and challenging your current beliefs, attitudes, assumptions, expectations and patterns of behavior in the manner shown. Take some time with this; it's very important to engage in self-awareness exercises to be able to see the changes you need to manage. Watch out for negative mind thoughts. Challenge them. But, how do you bring your thoughts up to a level of self-awareness that will enable you to make real change?

A helpful way is through using *psychological stems* from behavior modification exercises I've seen and tried. The Rotter Incomplete Sentences Blank (RISB) is the genesis for stems. For example, get a pen and paper and complete each of the following incomplete sentences with five answers (stems) for each and see what happens. I did the first one as an example only and you complete the rest. Do it spontaneously without too much thinking, i.e. write as rapidly as you can.

1. If I bring 5% more awareness today to my *relationships* with people, I will:
   - Listen with more care and attention
   - Understand the underlying needs each possesses
   - Show empathy with their legitimate concerns
   - Be sincere and professional in my communications
   - Follow-through on promises or implied commitments
2. If I bring 5% more awareness to my current *job performance,* I will: (list 5 stems).

3. If I bring 5% more awareness to what's *important in my career,* I will: (list another 5 stems)
4. If I am truly motivated to *move up in the organization,* I will: (another 5 stems)
5. If I am willing to *admit to my current weaknesses,* I will: (5 more)

If you do these exercises, you will see how the use of stems helps you to examine yourself so that you can break old habits and acquire new, more productive ones. These are only a few of the various stems you can use to examine your current behavior. There are more stems on the Web.

Chapter 18

Getting the Best from Consultants

Key Points from this Chapter:

1. *Finding a good consultant can help you reach your goals and offer value-for-value;*
2. *Rely on client-word-of-mouth when selecting a consultant and operate from clear Terms of Reference;*
3. *Value a long-term relationship because of the consultant's investment in your organization.*

If you reach an impasse on an important organizational problem and you know you need help, you may find yourself wondering about hiring an external consultant. You are paying for expertise, objectivity and confidentiality (like the consultant in Jane's case). Here are my thoughts on the subject that you can draw on if and when the need for consulting assistance arises.

1. There are hundreds of consultants out there. Choose one by word-of-mouth only and not by glossy brochures. Get references from clients directly, not from the consultant's boilerplate (marketing material).
2. Good consultants cost money. Be prepared to pay. Accept that up front.
3. You have a right to expect value for your money. Don't wait until the end of an assignment to express dissatisfaction or concern.

4. On the subject of money, you can often find big firm insight at a much lower cost from an independent consultant with the right experience and credentials.
5. You must work with the consultant, withholding neither information nor cooperation. They need to know your environment to be able to diagnose and recommend improvements.
6. Make sure the consultant's proposal, a.k.a. Terms of Reference, spells out (a) the expected deliverables i.e. measurable results; (b) program of work; and (c) time and fee estimate.
7. The consultant proposed to do the actual work must have a depth of experience in matters related to the assignment. Be certain to verify this because you are engaging this person's experience and not the firm's (which is not always the same unless it is a sole-practitioner).
8. Your key people must be made available to the consultant if needed. Their cooperation is a must.
9. Make sure you schedule feedback meetings at appropriate milestones during the assignment. Agree on these up-front.
10. Remember, you can terminate the consultant's services at anytime, paying only for the time spent on the assignment to-date.
11. Shop around for several consulting bids; it's better to have a choice of consultants, fee levels and work plans to compare the expected value.
12. If you're happy with the results of the work, keep this relationship going and be willing to refer your consultant to others. They will thank you.
13. Be realistic about implementing changes that flow from the consultant's advice. Introducing and managing agreed change can be complex as the previous chapters demonstrate. The organization has many interdependent parts that are affected by a change in even one part. Consider using the consultant to help plan and monitor the implementation phase. Deciding 'what' to change or improve is easy; but 'how' and 'by whom' the changes will be made affects roles, responsibilities and relationships where buy-in is critical.

A Case in Point: An Example of a Localized Organization Change Intervention.

Performance was lackluster in one of the departments of a government office. According to the Director, the employees were not productive and, worse, were showing their displeasure with constant complaints about conditions in the workplace and slowing their efforts just above a level that would otherwise get them disciplined. The Director finally chose an outside OC consultant after suitable checking for a reliable source. The employees were told of the decision to conduct an external, anonymous review with the objective of getting everyone's opinions on changes and improvements in the workplace. As expected, both management and staff held cynical opinions about the point of the exercise. Here's what the consultant did:

1. Met with groups of seven (minimum) to ten (maximum) employees guaranteeing anonymity to the information providers but making it very clear that the information collected would be public.
2. Asked the following questions, allowing each participant time to write personal own notes before group take-up.

   - On a scale of 1-10, how satisfied are you personally with the current conditions of work here?
   - What improvements, If they are feasible, do you feel are necessary to make? Please list two or three ideas, more if you like.
   - Why did you choose these? What problems will be solved? How will they help?
   - In addition to your thoughts, what do your colleagues generally consider to be weaknesses in the current operation?

The take-up of opinions in round-robin style, avoiding duplication of ideas, resulted in twenty distinct concerns. Each concern was viewed separately and clarification sought with answers provided by the author of the idea. Once the data were on view, individual participants were asked to choose the top 6 items to establish the group's priority. The meeting was adjourned.

The consultant met with the management group to whom the employees reported. They were shown the top 6 priorities, verbatim, given the employees' reasons and asked these questions:

1. Do you understand what the employees' top 6 priorities are, or do you want further clarification of their reasons for choosing this priority list?
2. If the points are understood, do you agree with these top priorities?
3. Which ones are you willing to act on and inform the employees accordingly?
4. How will you hold yourselves accountable to the group to ensure these changes are made?

Management was invited to choose changes in this order: (a) information gaps that could be answered immediately; (b) Policy statements that would shortly clarify requests for procedural clarity; and (c) changes that would respond, where feasible, to the organizational roadblocks that the employees had cited. Management was then asked to create a schedule of these changes and to publish it. The possibility of positive change had begun. The last step was to bring the employees together to receive feedback on the agreed changes and thanks for their participation. A key step was to reveal and discuss only the changes that were going to be implemented i.e. 'from now on we will' and deliberately omitting the original complaints that led to the employee recommendations. Why? Because there is no need to revert to another complaint session when the changes that employees wanted were already approved. The cost of this intervention was three days of the consultant's time and expertise. The value was cost savings and improved employee satisfaction because of their involvement in the decision process.

This example is only one of the services an external *organization* consultant can bring to the organization. I've discovered that a lot of potential leaders don't spend much time seeing if their own work climate enables people to do their best. Sometimes it takes an outside intervention to bring the employees' concerns to a level of awareness that causes top management action.

(On a personal note, sixty-to-seventy percent of my client work involved repeat business. That's another clue to consider when you are checking the references on your consulting short-list).

It's a pleasure to find and work with a good external consultant and vice-versa. He or she will be investing time getting familiar with your business and, after a time, will gain an understanding of your organization that can only be beneficial. As a final note, many organizations have internal consultants to assist you when needed. Use the same guidelines for choosing them.

Personal Exercise for Chapter 18

Store this chapter until you decide to seek a good consultant.

Chapter 19

Managing Cynicism

Key Points for this Chapter:

1. *Cynicism prevents you from operating with an open mind; neither does it help your credibility;*
2. *Healthy skepticism is okay as long as you eventually judge with informed opinion or facts;*
3. *You can manage your cynicism by relinquishing old truths and embracing new truths.*

How many times have you read a book or an article that focused on the rewards for personal development and thought, 'sounds appealing but . . .' (fill in the blanks) and laid it aside? I've read many books and articles and taken personal development workshops and courses all my life. I believe in continuous learning and what I have written in this book is mostly what I learned from others and a lot of personal reflection over my work experiences. Why the title of this chapter?

Cynicism means fault-finding and rationalizing. A cynic believes that human nature is motivated by self-interest which is one of the main contributors to false beliefs that leads to unrewarded behaviors. There are other definitions, of course, such as those who are excessively distrustful of human nature and especially the motives of others. I can remember having feelings like these; who hasn't? But, I learned that a great deal of my cynicism was grounded in false beliefs and, in the end, reflected poorly on me!

Cynics cling to old truths that keep them angry, irritated and unfulfilled. That leads to bitching as a way of rationalizing one's thoughts and actions. But, that just keeps you in the same mindset. And have you ever noticed that when a group of cynics join in a bitch session it spirals into finding all kinds of injustice in the workplace and the blame-game begins. Cynics express anger and dissatisfaction with plenty; they are not in a happy place. So what causes cynicism?

It seems to stem from a loss of sincere belief in oneself, one's relationships and one's outlook about the future. Was cynicism caused by past failure, broken trust, lack of recognition by people who mattered or some sense of inadequacy? One thing seems clear: *There are very few successful cynics!* By contrast, successful people show a lack of cynicism; to them the world owes them nothing. They go out and find what they want without asking permission. They are externalists who consider *themselves* the primary agents of change. They tend to focus on the positives of life, are optimistic about the future.

Chronic cynics, found in many organizations, don't trust in the honesty and intentions of others and harbor such false beliefs as: talent, usually their own, doesn't count; dedication doesn't guarantee anything; the system is built to screw you; it's who you know, not what you can do etc. Sound familiar? We could say that cynics are insecure people who lack belief in themselves and as a defense mechanism cope by blaming circumstances and others. Sadly, their belief system keeps their cynicism alive. In *Figure 33* is a Cynic Scale I read in one of the dailies (source lost) that gives a good overview of the nature of cynics. Take the test and see what you learn about your level of cynicism. Use the scale 1, 2, 3, 4 with 1=strongly disagree; and 4=strongly agree.

Figure 33: The Cynic Scale

---

1. Most people will tell a lie if they can gain from it.
2. People say they have ethical standards, but few stick to them when money is at stake.
3. People pretend to care more about others than they really do.
4. It's sad to see an unselfish person because so many people take advantage of them.
5. Most people are interested only in personal benefits.
6. Most people inwardly dislike helping other people.
7. Most people are really not honest by nature.

Now, add up the scores for your answers and consult the following legend.

Scoring

7-14 points: You are upbeat. Possibly too upbeat! You see people as caring, honest and loyal. Your optimism is a marker of good health; but beware; you might be an easy mark for cynics, liars and assorted swindlers. In short, you may be too trusting and suggestible.

15-20 points: You're a healthy skeptic. You tend to be wary until convinced otherwise, which is why you are making progress slowly but surely. One warning: your 'prove it first' attitude could be hurting your relationships. So, try to control your tendency to be suspicious of most things.

21-28 points: You're too cynical! You think people are selfish, self-serving, duplicitous and looking for an angle. You're too quick to watch your backside and are quick to take advantage of others if you think you can gain by it or before you believe they'll take advantage of you.

Does your score on this test give you a sense of your level of cynicism? When I read this test in a daily paper I asked a few peers to apply it to the employees where they worked. It didn't take long for them to identify individuals who bore these characteristics.

And guess what? Few of these people, if any, had ever received feedback on how they were perceived by others. So, how do you achieve a healthy balance of cynicism in the workplace? Examine the contrasting feelings shown in *Figure 34* and reflect on the message you get from it.

Figure 34: Breaking Cynicism

Working on Your Cynicism
Sample Thoughts for Examination

Typical Cynic's Thinking	Breaking the Cynic State
1. External events/circumstances determine my life.	I determine my future. I have no one to blame for failure but me.
2. The world owes me something.	I earn what I get so I stay focused on the positives.
3. I do the work; my boss ges the glory.	I can learn and grow and be a successful boss too.
4. All women/men are untrustworthy.	What is there about me that causes women/men to avoid me?
5. I'm smarter than the university kids they hire over me.	I have the talent and the opportunity to get my degree.
6. Life should be a lot easier than it is.	Life is difficult and full of challenges. Dealing with them will make me a stronger person.
7. I've never felt accepted by the "in crowd".	I have talents and the potential to excel and be accepted.
8. I don't see myself moving up the corporate ladder because of all the favouritism I see.	I have talents and the potential to excel and be accepted.
9. I guess I'll just have to "grin-and-bear-it" when negative events occur.	I reject surrender and non-reaction unless it is the best choice.
10. People are moving up ahead of me and they're no better than I am.	These people chose to move up and acted accordingly. I held back and allowed myself to be jealous. I can stop that.
11. Romance is great. Marriage eventually becomes a bore.	Marriage requires work. Love is an action. Am I being the kind of partner I should be?
12. I hate people who criticize me. I have names for them I can't repeat. Criticism sends me into a state of anxiety.	I can admit when I'm wrong and even apologize if appropriate. But I can ignore false statements and even confront the carriers.
13. I do things for others to make me look good.	I act because I want to, not because I have to.
14. I've never had any breaks.	I can prepare for breaks when they come along. The more prepared, the better the chances of success.

The point in this final chapter is to show how people can break old, harmful truths and replace them with new truths in order to prepare themselves to go up or out and up which is the theme of the book. As I reflect on the old truths I readily admit that I harbored those kinds of thoughts in my early career days. Thankfully, with education and good mentoring, I became sufficiently self-aware in time to make some important changes. Apart from all of the management concepts and human/social ideas in my book, in the end, *Making It in Management* will all come down to your mind-thoughts.

Personal Exercise for Chapter 19

Complete the cynic test *Figure 33*. Make a list of the truths that you carry in your mind that currently guide your behavior. If you find you possess cynical thinking similar to the negative examples in *Figure 34*, try to write a new truth for the negative thoughts and feelings that your listed items suggest. When you're finished, ask yourself, "What's in it for me if I operate from the new truths?" Or, conversely, ask yourself, "What's the worst thing that can happen to me if I accept and act on these new truths?" You can also try writing more stems as illustrated in Chapter 17.

Chapter 20

Deciding to Move *Up* or *Out?*

Key Points for this Chapter:

1. *You need feedback from above on your potential for upward moves; ask for it;*
2. *Judge for yourself whether the bosses above you are trustworthy i.e. they honor their word;*
3. *Deserve your promotion but start looking outside if you feel overlooked and exploited.*

As the title of my book presupposes, you will likely face the personal career decision to stay and go *up* in your present organization or go *out and up*. In either case, you are leveraging your accumulated management know-how to reap its value. You may choose to go out and up but remain in your industry; or you may decide to gain experience in a new business or industry; it's career progress, no matter which.

People who stayed with their organizations for most of their careers were once called *stabilizers*. Those who went out and up were once called *scramblers*. Once upon a time, people who moved around a lot were accused of being unstable. Now, it's a plus! So, how do you judge which way to go?

The real question to start the decision process is: Are my career needs being met here . . . and is there a good chance for personal betterment? Staying in and going up can be renewing, if the probability of promotion is high. Going out and up can also be renewing and even accelerate career advancement. In the latter case, the old adage, 'be careful what you ask for,' is good advice. There must be a compelling difference between the two opposites to help you make a decision. Here's an actual case to make my point.

One day, an inventory specialist came to my office in HR with a complaint. He claimed that his senior manager had said to him, "The next management position in the department is yours to lose." (This is a lousy and insensitive choice of words to a senior employee who is anxious to know his real chances for advancement!). When the competition was completed and a junior peer of the complainant was selected, the losing candidate was furious. The successful junior had no valid experience to match the man sitting in my office. I promised to investigate and I did.

Our company in this case had a Performance Appraisal system in place and I retrieved his file to review. The actual forms used each year had two distinct parts: Part A showed the actual job results and rating (positive or negative); while Part B was titled "Potential for Advancement." I did not know that Part B findings were not part of the performance feedback process. In fact, the Part B content was withheld specifically to avoid raising expectations! I didn't know that! I was new to the company. I innocently, and with good faith, laid out copies of the last four years of this man's appraisals on my desk and asked him to come to view them. All of the Part A's were satisfactory. No wonder he was curious at his static role in the department. But, in each successive year, Part B read, "Terminal in present position; not promotable."

When he arrived, I gave him all of the copies and left him to read them. Sitting outside my office, I heard him suddenly yell, "Son of a bitch," as he walked past me with papers in his hand, heading in the direction of his boss's office. My staff could hear him yelling as he walked down the hallway and out of sight. A few moments later he appeared in the hallway but this time he was wearing his coat. He yelled a suggestion that we all know is physically impossible. Then his manager appeared at my door with the Part B forms in his hand. "What the hell did you show him these for," he yelled. "Because you should have," I replied. Henceforth, Part B became part of the annual feedback process!

Fast forward six months. I met the former employee on the street one day. He stopped me with a smile and said, "I owe you one. If you hadn't shown me those documents, I'd have stayed with the company waiting my turn to move up. Now, I've got a great job in another company (which he named) in the same industry as the Inventory Manager . . . for a lot more money. Thank you."

So, what's the point of the story? Plateaus are bound to occur if you stay put. Responsibilities may remain static for periods longer than you'd hoped. But you've got to get some sense from above about your career possibilities. If the news isn't positive, you can use your current position as a safety net while you look elsewhere for opportunities. The grass may look greener on the outside so make sure you are not leaving for the wrong reasons. If you're at your peak and there's nowhere else to go where you are maybe a move is the wisest choice. If so, being risk-averse by nature is important. And if you have good experience and track record, chances of improving your opportunities are positive.

Personal Exercise for Chapter 20

This is a good opportunity to take stock of your strengths and weaknesses as they apply to moving up in your current organization. Look back over the duration of your employment with this organization, and others. Answer the following questions with a lot of reflection and maybe with input from others you trust or stakeholders, like family, who will be affected by your change.

1. Do I really want to move up or out and up, or is this just a thought at this time?
2. Am I being realistic about my qualifications and experience to move up?
3. What criteria can I use to decide if moving up is really what I want?
4. Do I trust my boss to give me honest feedback on my potential and chances for promotion?
5. Can I count on my boss's sponsorship?
6. If I have reservations about my current abilities to move up, what are they?
7. Can I make those needed changes?
8. To get what I think I want, what will I have to give up or lose?
9. Have I received clear signals from my peers that I am promotable?
10. Do I aspire to become a member of the senior team? Are they a cohesive and ethical group I truly respect?
11. What are the costs/benefits of moving up or out and up?
12. What's the worst thing that can happen to me if I stay where I am? Is that okay?
13. Am I confident enough *not* to fear failure?
14. What is there about me that I will have to change?
15. Is going up what I really value?

By the time you process these questions and get feedback from others, you'll intuitively know what to do.

Summary

My purpose in writing ***Making It in Management*** is to share organization concepts and techniques that will increase an aspiring manager's chances for upward mobility. I have witnessed enough successes and failures in the workplace to conclude that *knowledge of how an organization works* becomes more important the higher one moves up the corporate ladder. There are countless management topics for self-study and self-development but learning to work *on* and not just *in* your organization is at the top of my list. Here's a summary of the main points I've tried to pass on in each chapter.

1. ***The Purpose of Your Organization***: The management process begins with a conceptual understanding of the big picture, i.e. *the organization's purpose*. A manager with this perspective, who can explain 'why' the organization exists and 'what' key business results are essential for success, is an asset to the organization. This top-down perspective enables managers to align their goals, accordingly. Likewise, a conceptual understanding of the key management functions that cause corporate results enables managers to focus their energy and resources wisely.

2. ***How Your Organization Should Work:*** The primary organizational elements that make up an "organization" are *Strategy, Structure, Processes, People, Climate and Culture.* Keeping these interdependent elements healthy and functioning is a primary example of a manager working *on* and not just in her or his organization. Aspiring managers must be competent in optimizing the performance of these organizational variables.

3. ***Your Job as Manager:*** Each management position has a purpose and expected key results. Clarifying the *Key Responsibility Areas* (KRAs) of a manager's job in terms of the *actual* results to be achieved, defines the manager's specific contribution to the organization.

4. ***Multiple Roles You Must Know How to Play:*** Managers need to master a variety of diverse *roles* to achieve their expected Key Results. Within the eight primary managerial roles shown in this chapter, are twenty-four critical skills that managers require to showcase their personal effectiveness. This skill list is a basis for continuing self-development.

5. ***What Having Credibility Means for You:*** Your personal credibility dictates the degree to which people are attracted to you, accept you and willingly follow you. The word "credibility" implies *believability*. Your believability is grounded in the perceptions others have of you (not your self-perception) and influences the nature and quality of your work relationships. As abstract a term as *credibility* is, everyone you know you has opinions about you. This demands self-awareness and self-control on your part.

6. ***Creating Strategy:*** A manager is expected to provide direction to a unit within the context of the direction given from above. The SWOT process is an excellent tool to master for creating strategy; likewise, skill in formulating the unit's plan Mission, Values and Goals will enable managers to provide focus for unit performance.

7. ***Providing Structure:*** Managers need to provide *structure* for guiding organizational behavior. This means experimenting with roles, reporting relationships, job content, methods and procedures, policies and procedures. Learning to distinguish between and measure both *effectiveness* and *efficiency* will lead to business improvements.

8. ***Use Processes that Drive Efficiency:*** *How* work is done affects efficiency. Finding the 'best' ways to perform the work is achieved through regular monitoring of process efficiencies and engaging employees in suggesting improvements. Finding newer, better and faster ways of doing tasks with fewer resources is a benefit that gets noticed from above.

9. ***Enabling Others to Want to do Their Best***: What is 'human resource management' anyway? The elements shown in the *Human Resource Development Process* in Chapter 9 provide a good template for enabling a manager to successfully *attract, develop and retain* good people. The eleven processes, collectively, add up to a holistic human resource approach for managers who want to be noted for their people skills.

10. ***Managing Human Resource Performance Challenges***: Influencing others to *want to* do their best is one of the biggest challenges for managers. How does a manager motivate people? Expecting people to act in ways that serve your values is unrealistic, even naïve. But getting them to *want to do* what you want them to do is more easily achieved by placing the perception in their minds that what you *expect* will also serve their values. The *Expectancy Theory of Motivation* illustrates a practical approach to motivation using an employee's values as the key to getting a willing response. Likewise, using an established feedback model like the "I-Language" technique shown is another key to behavior change.

11. ***Maintaining a Great Work Climate***: The importance of *work climate* becomes critical once it is viewed from the employees' perspective. "Climate is the workplace as perceived by the employees (not the manager)." Employee evaluations of existing *workplace conditions* and their ideas for change will lead to improvements that enable people to do their best. The aim is to have the employees consider their unit to be a "great place" to work.

12. ***Living Core Values:*** The publication and use of "values" sends a strong message about what behaviors will or won't be supported within the organization. Great companies operate on clear, strong, ethical values. Writing a values statement for your unit and measuring compliance to it on a regular basis contributes greatly to responsible performance. This chapter illustrates simple ways to do this.

13. ***Learning to Learn to Learn***: Learning is a process and learning to learn from experience is an essential part of the management process. The *Experiential Learning Model* illustrated in the chapter shows how regular and systematic

debriefing of completed work cycles leads to ideas for more efficient ways to work in future similar situations.

14. ***Advocating Well-Managed Change***; Managing change is an essential part of manager's job and a critical skill, as well. The processes in this chapter show how lasting change can be implemented with efficiency, simplicity and employee support.

15. ***Finding a Good Mentor***: Mentors can accelerate your career progress . . . if you get a good one. But good mentors are scarce and, as a rule, you don't find them; they find you. You *attract* a good mentor when they see qualities in you that they value and feel they possess. Your strong performance is an entry requirement. Good character is assumed. Your perceived potential is a key condition for being noticed by a good mentor. (Do not overlook the mentoring value of the many practical management books on the market).

16. ***Managing Your Boss:*** Approach this requirement with a few givens: your boss plays an important role in your future advancement. He or she has a different level of responsibility than you and a host of problems different than yours. He or she has connections to key people above you and can become your advocate. For this essential support, you need to perform your responsibilities in an exemplary manner and, equally important, you need to be a key factor in your boss's success. If you can take on some of your boss's current responsibilities it will show support while giving you the chance to acquire higher-level skills.

17. ***Mastering Your Mind Thoughts:*** If the results of your behavior, over time, are not meeting your needs, the way you think (your values, beliefs, attitudes and expectations) may need examination. Replacing 'old truths' with new ones can be a turning point for aligning your behavior with your needs. Your mind thoughts can be an enemy or a friend. In this chapter are techniques for raising your self-awareness to enable you to better meet your needs.

18. ***Getting the Best from Consultants:*** There's a time and place when a good consultant will be of great benefit. How to choose one is critical. Good consultants are expensive and

you have a right to expect results. The tips in this chapter will show you how to find and get the best results from a qualified consultant. If you choose wisely, the relationship will provide value-for-value for an indefinite time.

19. ***Managing Cynicism:*** *The way you think determines the way you act.* If you are cynical about others—your managers, peers and employees—and your trust level is low, the tips in the chapter will help get you out of a rut that, unless corrected, will cause irreparable harm and keep you from realizing your full potential. Re-programming your thinking will open your mind to new possibilities and rid you of the limited thinking that is holding you back.

20. ***Deciding Whether to Move Up or Out and Up:*** If you possess the conceptual and hard skills outlined in my book, you are on your way! These, alone, should qualify you for a higher-level position. But, the question about staying where you are and going up, or going outside and up, depends on your answers to some very tough questions as shown in the chapter. It's a good idea to sit down and answer these questions spontaneously (without too much 'thinking') to put your future in perspective. Your answers should enable you to make the right conclusion.

In the above chapters I have eagerly put my mentoring hat on because I have had a fulfilling thirty-five year career in management consulting (a uniquely satisfying one) and I want to pass on some practical tips and techniques that I learned through self-development and great mentoring. I sincerely hope that the content has enlightened you and that you have discovered new ideas to add to your current assets. You'll notice that nothing is mentioned in my book about your *technical* skills. That is the base on which your career started. But, the world of management has unique challenges beyond your technical know-how; thus my choice of topics is about conceptual knowledge of how your organization works; it is the basis for a successful management career.

You are in far more control of your career than you imagine. I believe that when you master the main concepts and skills described in the book, positive change will happen. I chose the chapters and content carefully from among all the other possible topics in management because they are the ones that are barely touched-upon in university studies. Nor were they consistently practiced by people holding management positions in the organizations where I worked and still consult. That's why deeper knowledge of organizational behavior has always kept my interest high and reinforces my beliefs when I witness credible managers modeling these organizational practices while earning respect and achieving success for their organizations and themselves.

I wish you good fortune in your management career and hope you conclude that my attempt at vicarious mentoring to be one that helps you move in the direction you really want to go. Bon Voyage.

Lawrence Anderson, Vancouver, Canada

Acknowledgements

Over the course of a 35-year organizational consulting career, I took and taught courses, read countless management books, attended professional seminars and asked acknowledged experts the kinds of questions I've tried to address in this book. A lot of information came my way live and in print. Good mentoring added to my knowledge base and consulting on over one hundred organizational assignments kept my learning curve pointed skywards. I want to acknowledge as many sources as I can who contributed to my understanding of organization change. I am listing the main sources mentioned in the book as best I can remember and in case I have forgotten to give credit to an important source I hope to be forgiven for my inability to recall important sources. Below are the primary sources I have mentioned in the book that were influential in forming the body of knowledge I have been fortunate to acquire. I recommend you consult (e.g. Google) these sources to get more information and a deeper understanding of their message and reference sources.

Chapters

1: The Purpose of Your Organization

Tom Peters and Richard Waterman ignited my interest in what makes organizations excellent in their classic book, *In Search of Excellence.*

Jim Collin's books, *Good to Great* and *Built to Last*, did the same.

MacLean's magazine (October 2010) featured the article about the success of Canada's WestJet that seemed to fit this chapter.

Fortune magazine's annual "Best 100 Companies" report is a great source of models of corporate excellence.

3: Your Job as Manager

Malcolm Gladwell's *Outliers* demonstrates the fallibility of overnight success in getting to the top.

George Odiorne of the University of Michigan wrote great articles and facilitated impressive workshops I had the pleasure to attend on the use of KRA's and MBO.

4: The Multiple Roles You Must Know How to Play

Robert Quinn of the University of Michigan wrote *Beyond Rational Management* which piqued my interest and became a staple in my learning approach in workshops for managers.

5: What Having Credibility Means to You

The work of Daniel Goleman of Harvard in *Working with Emotional Intelligence* provided a sound base for identifying and developing people with emotional maturity. I find it invaluable for recruiting and developing managers.

Likewise, the authors of the Johari Window opened the possibilities of developing self-awareness.

6: Creating Strategy

The *Harvard Business Review* (HBR) is always a strong source of information on current happenings in the management world. Their article in April 2008 on the emergence and growth of *Edward Jones* financial planners is an excellent illustration of developing business strategy.

7: Providing Structure

As an academic teaching Organization Behavior, I discovered the work of Hackman and Oldham and their impressive work on the structuring of jobs to increase productivity and job satisfaction.

9: Managing Others to Want to Do Their Best

Henry Mintzberg of McGill has contributed greatly to my understanding of a manager's role.

10: Human Performance Challenges

Chuck Dwyer of the Wharton School was very influential in explaining the dynamics of the Expectancy Theory of Motivation.

Manuel P. Smith's book, *When I Say 'No.' I Feel Guilty*, teaches verbal problem-solving skills that really do increase a manager's assertiveness and credibility.

Frederick Hertzberg's work on the *Hygiene Theory of Motivation* still has appeal in considering motivation and climate factors.

Ken Blanchard's classic, *The One-Minute Manager*, proved the value and importance of timely and specific feedback.

Thomas and Kilmann's work in *Dealing with Conflict* is classic material all managers need to visit and embrace.

The thoughts on time management and avoiding self-assumed heroism came from hilarious HBR article 99609

11: Maintaining a Great Work Climate

Korn Ferry occasionally publishes helpful articles for clients, among which was the one particular survey referred-to emphasizing the importance of workplace climate.

Google provides numerous sources (Great Places to Work)

12: Defining and Living Core Values

From Will Schutz, an OD consultant, I got insight into consensus decision-making and the rules for achieving it made a big difference to my facilitating skills. He is a strong contributor to the field of Organization Development.

14: Advocating Well-managed Change

Robert Quinn, mentioned in chapter four, is a key resource for brokering organizational change.

17: Mastering Your Mind Thoughts

The source of psychological stems comes from the Rotter Incomplete Sentence Blank.

Conclusion: It is impossible to recall all of the sources of my accumulated learning about organization change. Suffice to say, I learned a great deal from others as well as through my own successes and failures. My thanks to my teachers, in whatever form they took—animate and inanimate, for a deeply-satisfying career . . . and my apologies if I have overlooked giving others credit where credit is due.

Finally, I want to thank two very special people: my wife Carol for whom the book is dedicated (and who keeps me grounded) and our very good friend Barbara Waigh whose English skills and diligence caught my spelling and grammatical mistakes before they reached the publisher and exposed my shortcomings.

Lawrence Anderson

Vancouver, Canada www.ocpartner.com